THE BROWN'S SYSTEM TEACHES

ETIQUETTE AND SOCIAL BEHAVIOR

THE BROWN'S SYSTEM TEACHES

ETIQUETTE AND SOCIAL BEHAVIOR

BY

DR. DORIS J. BROWN

Copyright © 1996, 2000 by Dr. Doris J. Brown

All rights reserved. No part of this book may be reproduced, stored in a retrieval system, or transmitted by any means, electronic, mechanical, photocopying, recording, or otherwise, without written permission from the author.

ISBN: 1-58500-610-6

This book is printed on acid free paper

1st Books rev. 11/07/00

ABOUT THE BOOK

This is a wonderful book that has been designed to share some skills to children and the entire family on Etiquette and social behavior. Learning good social skills is a wonderful way to bring everybody together for a common goal. Being able to show Respect, Grace, and Thankfulness are good gestures to have. Table manors, and learning how to eat are key elements that young and old can benefit from. Please allow this book to be a part of your children's etiquette life and also allow this book to be a part of your adult life as well. Reading this book will help us all young and old to think GOOD THOUGHTS.

Good etiquette and social behavior skills is good for your children, family, and friends to learn EVERY ONE WORKS TOGETHER "ON THIS ONE".

THIS IS THE UNITED STATES OF AMERICA IS A GOOD COUNTRY

PLEDGE ALLEGIANCE TO THE FLAG OF AMERICA

I PLEDGE ALLEGIANCE TO THE FLAG
OF THE UNITED STATES OF AMERICA
AND TO THE REPUBLIC FOR WHICH IT
STANDS, ONE NATION, UNDER GOD, INDIVISIBLE,
WITH LIBERTY AND JUSTICE FOR ALL.

"A GOOD STORY OF GOOD
by DR. DORIS J. BROWN A GOOD PERSON"

I like to do good things and see good things happen for people all the time. My good things to do when I was younger, and still today is to go to school, carnival, circus, and to the zoo. I would go to all of these places so that I could feed the animals.

The wonderful state of Tennessee was my home and where I lived with my other sisters and brothers. The carnival would come to the Southgate Shopping Center each and every year. The first time I went to the carnival was at the age of three years old. My last trip to the carnival in Memphis, Tennessee was when I was 18 years old. When I turned 18 years old, I had to move away to attend college to further my education.

The carnival would bring Fun and the food was very good; I would eat corn dogs, cotton candy, pop corn, and candy apples. I would eat so much that I was sick the next day but I still had to go to school. While visiting the carnival I saw several types of animals. Their were <u>Pony Rides</u> and <u>Elephant Rides</u>. Each year the price would increase.

Disappointed

Remember the Pony's and Elephant's were riding all the people at the Shopping Center. When I turned eight (8) years old I was ready for my elephant ride. I asked my mother if I could take a ride, she told me that she did not have enough money, I started crying very hard because I wanted my elephant ride. I sat on a bench in front of the Katz Drug store and continued crying because I wanted to ride the elephant.

Cassie the Elephant looked at me while I was crying so hard. I started walking over to the elephant while I was crying. I said "CASSIE I WANT TO RIDE BUT I DO NOT HAVE ANY MONEY" The elephant lifted me with his trunk, picked me up and placed me on his head. I was so happy that my tears stopped. I felt very good and I learned the elephant cared because I was kind, gentle, and treated her good for all those years that I visited the carnival.

The leader of the elephant's told me that Cassie liked me as a friend and would not harm me because I cared about her. Please be nice, warm, and friendly all the time.

GOOD CAME TO ME BECAUSE I WAS A GOOD PERSON

THE END

"THINK GOOD THINGS"

One day my mother took myself and the other family members to the Southgate Shopping Center for shopping. The carnival had arrived three (3) days early. The carnival was open and all the people looked like they were having fun. I looked and saw the Elephants and I thought that they were cute and cuddly.

Joyful

The elephants look so pretty in their outfits, they were just riding people around the carnival. I wanted to ride the elephant so bad but I did not have any money. I walked over to the elephant and asked for a ride. I started talking to the elephant, I was six (6) years old at the time my first question was

WHY ARE YOU SO BIG

He did not say anything to me back so I knew at that time that the elephant could not talk. My mother came out of the drug store screaming because she saw me playing with the very large animal. I told my mother to be quite because I made a friend, with a big animal. The elephant's name was **CASSIE** her skins was very dry and she needed some lotion. I told Cassie that I would be a friend.

THINGS TO DO AT HOME TO HELP MOM AND DAD

When mom and dad work all day and sometimes all night to help make more money to provide for your needs, you can help them out by being good and doing things. Please do not look in **DISBELIEF** you really can make a difference and do something good.

Disbelieving

GOOD ALWAYS COMES when you help your family to be happy. You can always help out around the house, by cleaning your room and cleaning yourself. The **TRASH CAN** must be used at all times. Use the trash can all the time instead of leaving things on the **FLOOR**, on your **BED**, and all over the **HOUSE**. **PLEASE USE THE TRASH CAN FOR ALL THE WASTE THAT YOU DO NOT WANT. DO NOT LEAVE YOUR THINGS SUCH AS CLOTHES, TOYS, AND PAPER LAYING AROUND THE HOUSE.**

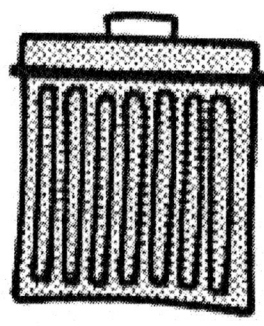

TRASH CAN

A SPECIAL LIST OF GOOD THINGS YOU CAN DO

    You must take special care of your clothes, all of your clothes must be placed on a clothes hanger a clothes hanger looks like this:

WATER PAIL

When you plant some flowers and trees around the house and in the yard, they must have water to live. You need to use a water pail to water the plants and flowers: A water pail looks like this:

NEWSPAPER

When mom and dad bring a Newspaper home ask them to read the paper so you can learn about the world. A newspaper looks like this:

I can keep my room clean with these very special things they are a Broom and a Vacuum Cleaner. A broom and a vacuum looks like this:

BROOM

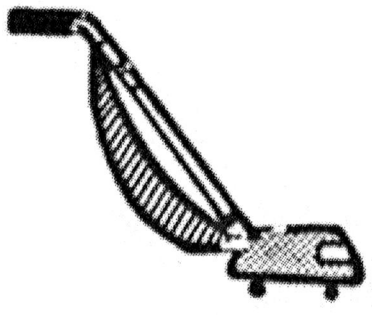

VACUUM CLEANER

GOOD AND HELPFUL THINGS TO DO WHEN USING EATING TOOLS

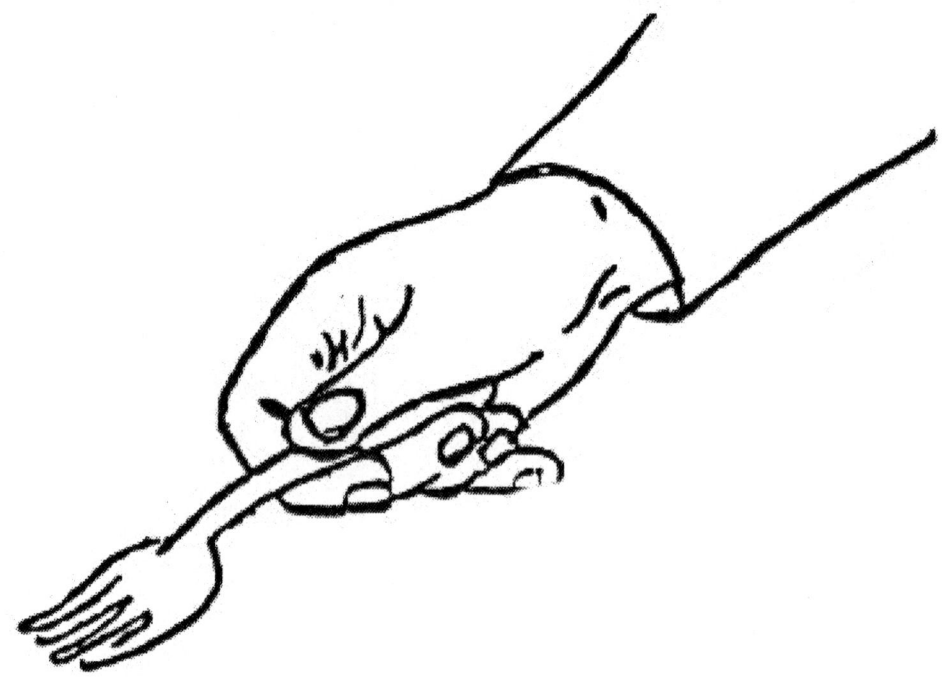

YOU MUST USE A FORK TO EAT WITH, WHEN HANDLING FLATWARE TOUCH ONLY THE HANDLES.

GOOD AND HELPFUL THINGS TO DO WHEN USING EATING TOOLS

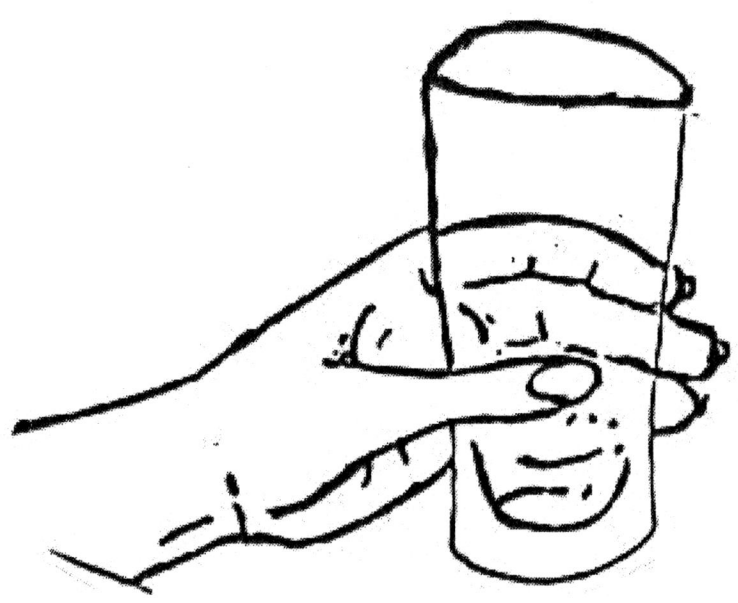

YOU MUST DRINK OUT OF A GLASS, WHEN HANDLING A GLASS TOUCH ONLY THE BASE OR LOWER PART, NEVER THE RIM.

GOOD AND HELPFUL THINGS TO DO WHEN USING EATING TOOLS

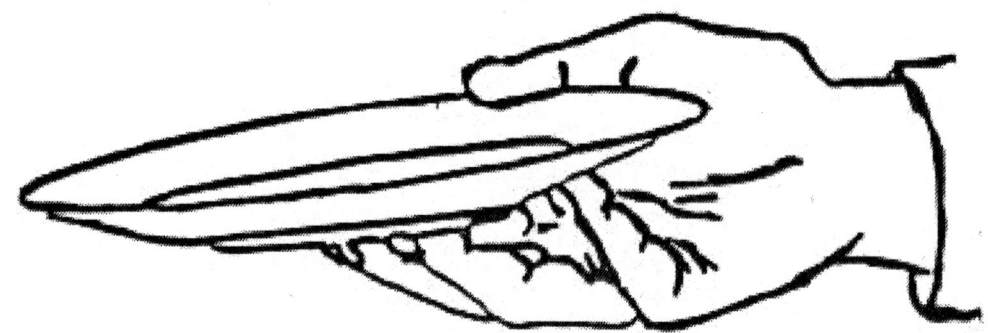

YOU MUST EAT YOUR FOOD ON A PLATE, WHEN HANDLING OR SERVING PLATES, TOUCH ONLY THE RIMES, THIS IS A GOOD BEHAVIOR TO USE AT ALL TIMES.

SETTING THE TABLE USING A TABLECLOTH

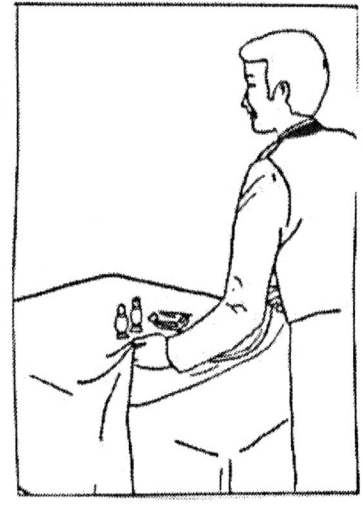

THESE ARE THREE WAYS FOR POSTIONING A TABLECLOTH
(1) THE FOLD IS PLACED IN THE CENTER OF THE TABLE.
(2) THE CLOTH IS OPENED AND GATHERED AT THE CENTER OF THE TABLE, WHILE THE SALT AND PEPPER SHAKERS ARE MOVED TO THE HALF THAT HAS ALREADY BEEN EXTENDED OUT.
(3) THE TABLECLOTH IS THEN PLACED OVER THE REMAINDER OF THE TABLE FROM THE OPPOSITE SIDE.

FLATWARE

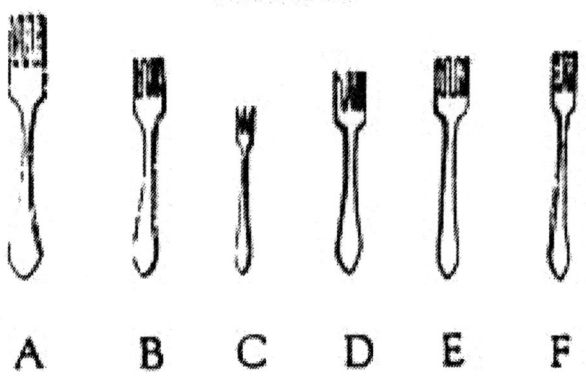

(A) DINNER
(B) SALAD
(C) OYSTER
(D) FISH
(E) DESSERT
(F) FRUIT

FLATWARE

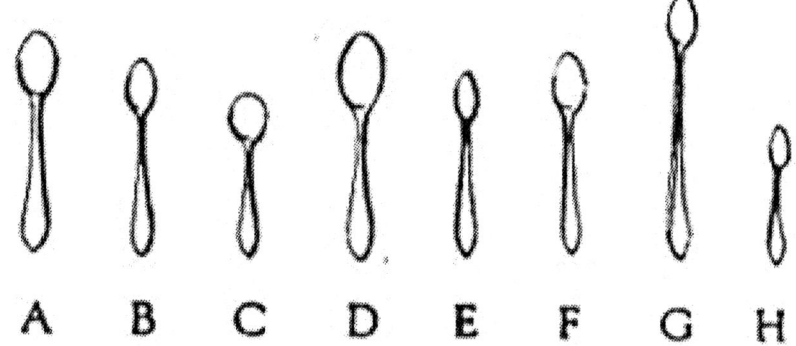

(A) DINNER SPOON
(B) TEASPOON
(C) CONSOMME SPOON
(D) SOUP SPOON
(E) GRAPEFRUIT SPOON
(F) DESSERT SPOON
(G) ICED TEA SPOON
(H) DEMITASSE SPOON

FLATWARE

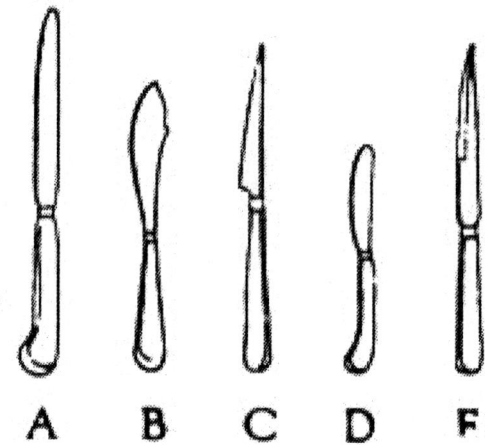

(A) DINNER KNIFE
(B) FISH KNIFE
(C) STEAK KNIFE
(D) BUTTER KNIFE
(E) FRUIT KNIFE

TABLE SETTING AMERICAN DISPLAY

BREAKFAST AND LUNCH SETTING

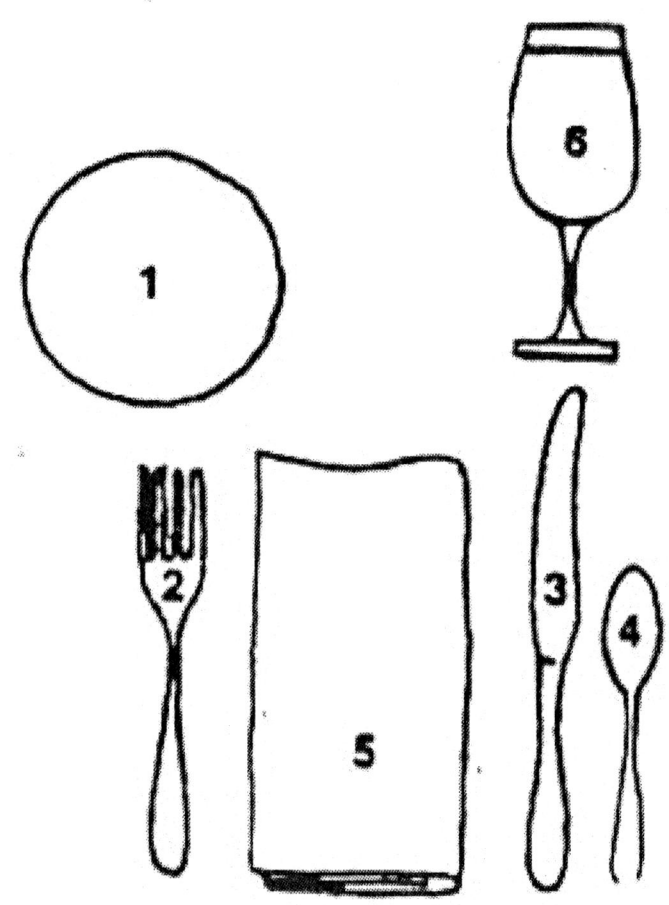

IN THE AMERICAN BREAKFAST AND LUNCH DISPLAY THESE ITEMS ARE USED:
(1) BREAD-and-BUTTER PLATE
(2) DINNER FORK
(3) DINNER KNIFE
(4) TEASPOON
(5) NAPKIN
(6) WATER GLASS

TABLE SETTING AMERICAN DISPLAY

BREAKFAST AND LUNCH SETTING

WHEN YOU SIT DOWN TO EAT AND THE TABLE IS SET, FOR AMERICAN BREAKFAST AND LUNCH, THE DISHES ARE PLACED IN SPECIFIC LOCATIONS. FOLLOW THIS DISPLAY.
(1) PLATE FOR BREAKFAST TOAST OR LUNCHEON SALAD
(2) ENTREE PLATE
(3) CUP AND SAUCER

TABLE SETTING AMERICAN DISPLAY (DINNER)

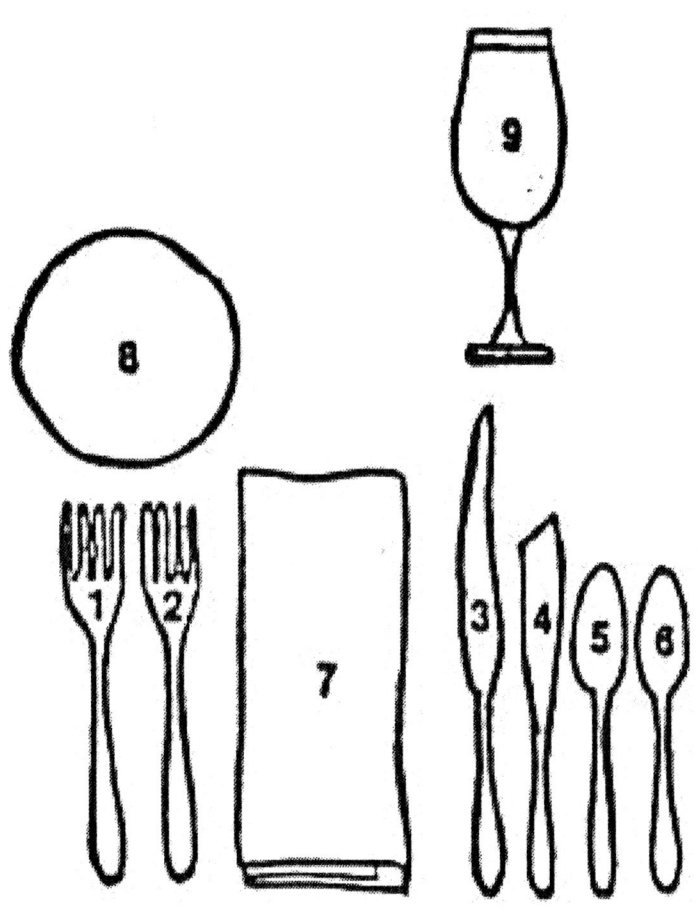

THE AMERICAN DINNER COVER IS SET AS FOLLOWS:

(1) SALAD FORK
(2) DINNER FORK
(3) DINNER KNIFE
(4) BUTTER SPREADER
(5) DINNER SPOON
(6) TEASPOON
(7) NAPKIN
(8) BREAD-and-BUTTER PLATE
(9) WATER GLASS

TABLE SETTING AMERICAN DISPLAY (DINNER)

WHEN THE MEAL IS SERVED USING THE AMERICAN DINNER COVER, THE DISHES ARE ADDED AS FOLLOWS:
(1) SALAD PLATE
(2) SERVICE PLATE
(3) CUP AND SAUCER

TABLE SERVICE

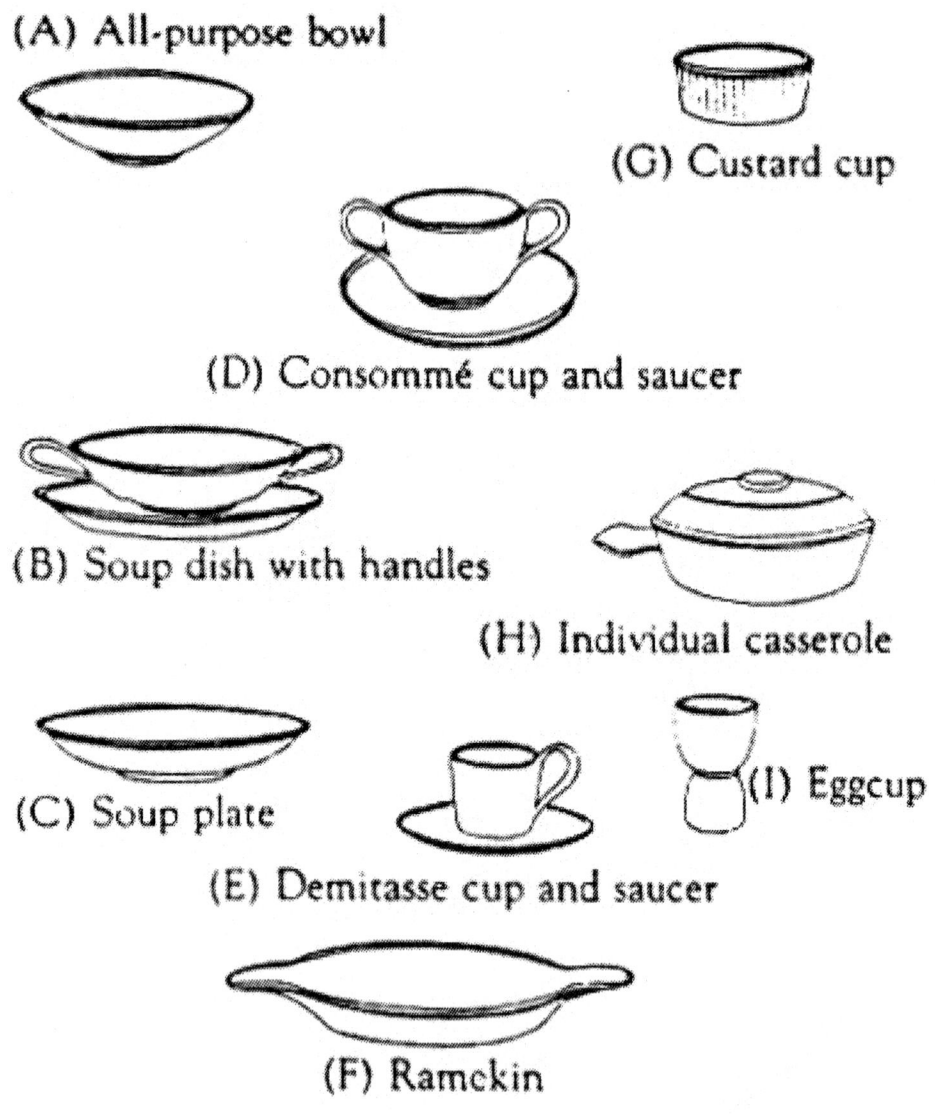

TABLE SERVICE

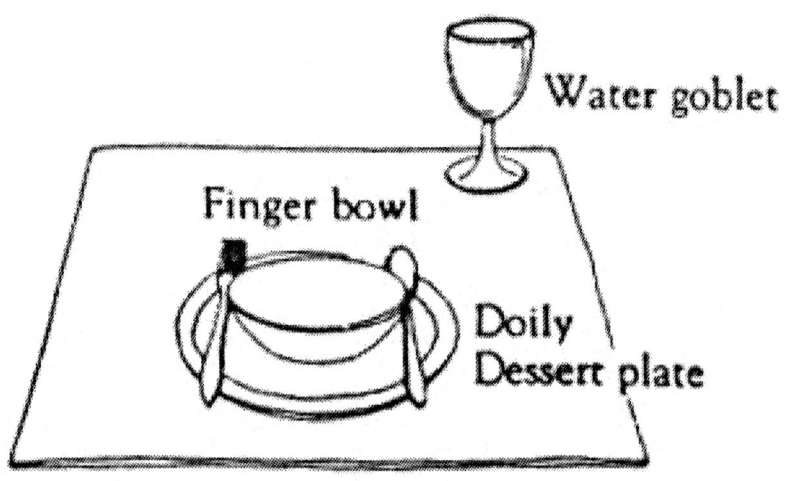

    THE FINGER BOWL and the custom of washing one's hands before and sometimes after eating is ancient. The Romans and Egyptians were meticulous about this. The finger bowl in its present appeared around the fifteenth century on the King of Sicily's dinner table.

SOUP FOR A LUNCHEON

SOMETIMES WHEN YOU EAT LUNCH YOUR SOUP WILL BE SERVED IN A CUP LIKE THIS. YOU CAN EAT YOUR SOUP WITH A SOUP SPOON OR DRINK BY LIFTING THE CUP.

SOUP FOR DINNER

THIS SOUP IS BEING SERVED IN A BOWL

THIS SOUP IS BEING SERVED IN A BOWL

IT IS A GOOD IDEA TO TAKE THE SOUP SPOON AND DIP IT INTO THE BOWL REST SPOON ON THE EDGE OF THE BOWL, SO THAT THE SOUP WILL NOT DRIP BRING SPOON TO YOUR MOUTH TO EAT SOUP.

HOW TO USE FLATWARE

PUT FORK IN YOUR LEFT HAND USING THE LEFT INDEX FINGER MAKE SURE TO PUSH THE HANDLE OF YOUR FORK INTO THE FOOD. HOLD YOUR KNIFE WITH YOUR RIGHT HAND USING THE INDEX FINGER TO CUT YOUR FOOD.
ONCE YOU HAVE CUT A PIECE OF FOOD LAY THE KNIFE ACROSS THE OUTER RIGHT-HAND SIDE OF YOUR PLATE WITH THE CUTTING EDGE FACING THE OUTSIDE OF YOUR MEAL. RETURN FORK TO YOUR RIGHT HAND TO PLACE FOOD INTO YOUR MOUTH.

WHEN YOU ARE RESTING BETWEEN BITES OF FOOD LEAVE YOUR KNIFE AND FORK ON YOUR PLATE LIKE THIS.

GOOD EATING MANNERS ARE VERY IMPORTANT

WHEN YOU ARE FINISHED EATING YOUR MEAL PLACE YOUR FORK AND KNIFE ON YOUR PLATE LIKE THIS.

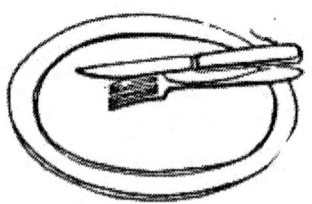

GOOD TABLE MANNERS

THIS IS A PICTURE OF POOR TABLE MANNERS

NEVER EAT LEANING BACKWARDS, YOU COULD WASTE YOUR FOOD AND SITTING LIKE THIS MAKES IT VERY HARD TO CHEW YOUR FOOD PROPERLY.

LEARN HOW TO FOLLOW DIRECTIONS

"BUT DO NOT PUT THE SPOON BACK IN THE POT"

LEARN HOW TO FOLLOW DIRECTIONS

WHEN YOU CLEAN DON'T JUST MOVE THE DIRT FROM SIDE TO SIDE

"REALLY CLEAN IT UP"

GOOD BEHAVIOR: GOOD BEHAVIOR: GOOD (BEHAVIOR)

When mom or dad expects me to sit down and relax I try to use a Chair. This is a good chair to sit down in and relax and study or watch Television. This is a good Chair:

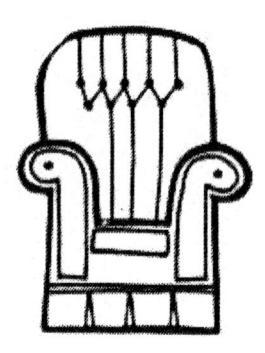

I have to sleep sometime and I have to wake up on time so that I can get to school. If I do not use a Clock I would sleep to long and all day. A Clock is what I need in my room and all over the House. This is a Clock:

CLOCK

TELEPHONE TECHNIQUES

THESE ARE SOME GOOD SKILLS TO USE WHEN YOU START TALKING ON THE TELEPHONE

- SPEAK CLEARLY IN THE RECEIVER.
- DO NOT SHOUT ON THE TELEPHONE.
- TAKE A MESSAGE IF THE PERSON IS NOT AVAILABLE TO TAKE THE CALL.
- ALWAYS BE KIND AND POLITE.
- SAY THANK YOU VERY MUCH.
- IF THEY HAVE A ANSWERING MACHINE, LEAVE A SHORT MESSAGE FOR THE PERSON YOU CALLED ON THE ANSWERING MACHINE.

LEARN TO BE GOOD AND THINK GOOD THINGS ALL THE TIME

HAVE FUN FOLDING NAPKINS YOU CAN HELP SET THE TABLE WITH SOME OF THESE DIFFERENT TYPES OF NAPKINS.

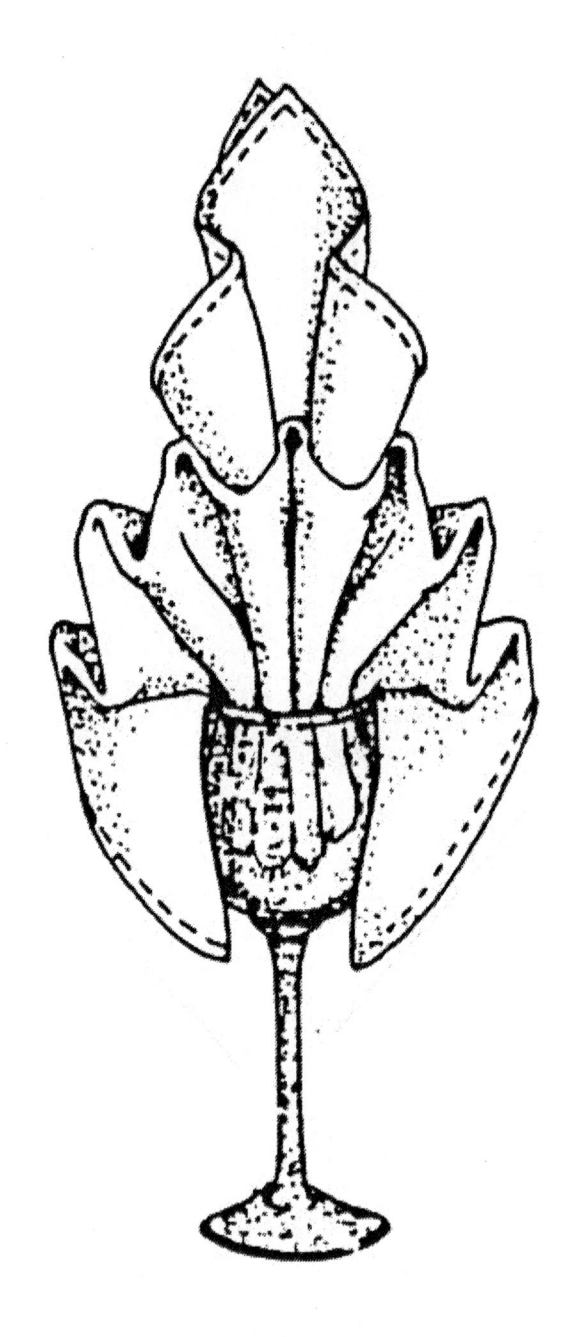

HAVE FUN

Graduation

The Flat Sachet

1. Fold the napkin into thirds.

2. Fold the top flap back in quarters twice to form a band across the middle of the napkin.

3. Turn the napkin over and fold back each side one quarter.

4. Fold each side again to meet in the center.

5. Fold in half with the right side under the left side.

6. Pull the center of the first flap back with your finger, creating a small diamond with a slit down the middle, and tuck the bottom of the diamond under the band.

7. Repeat with the other end and lay the napkin flat.

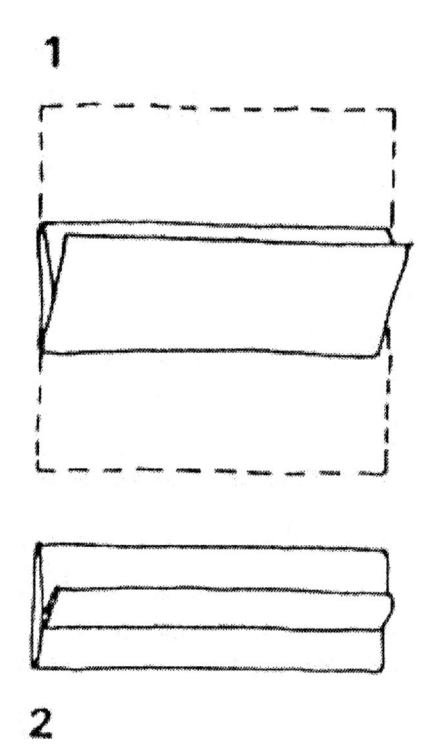

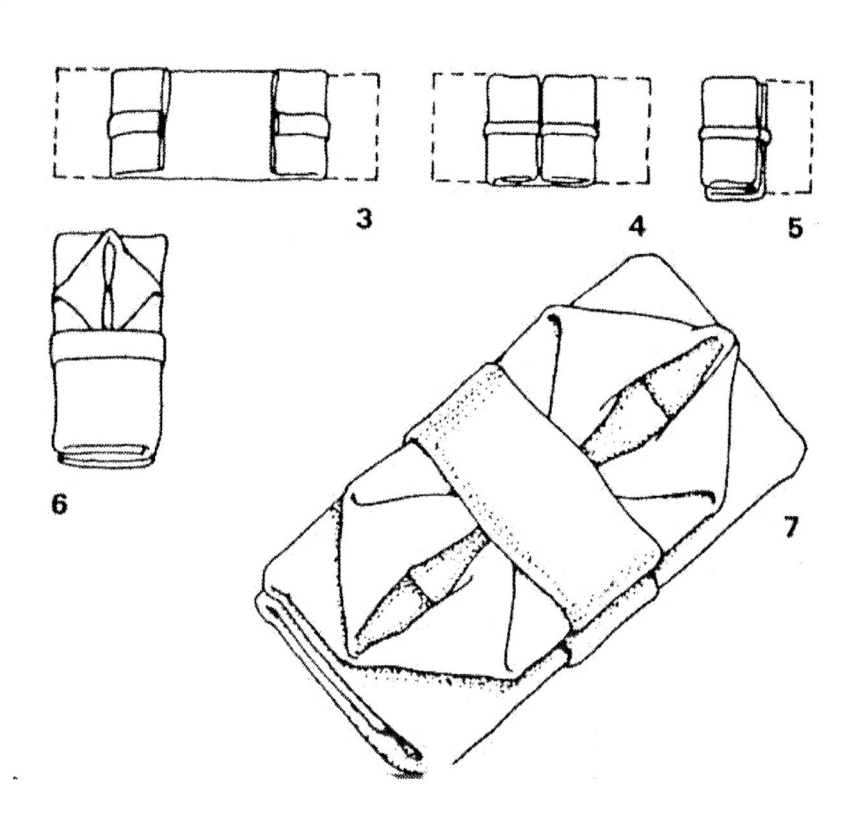

Breakfast

THE WAND

1. Fold all 4 corners to the center.
2. Fold the napkin in half.
3. Fold in half again.
4. Fold into thirds.
5. Fold in half and slip through a napkin ring.
6. Turn down the first flap at the top.

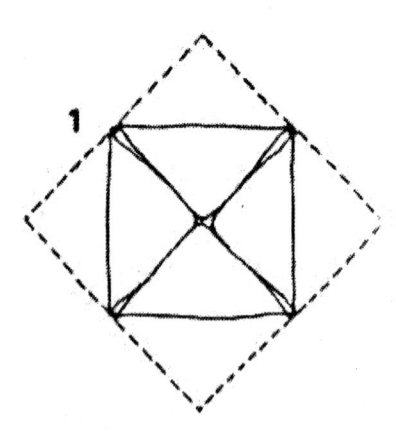

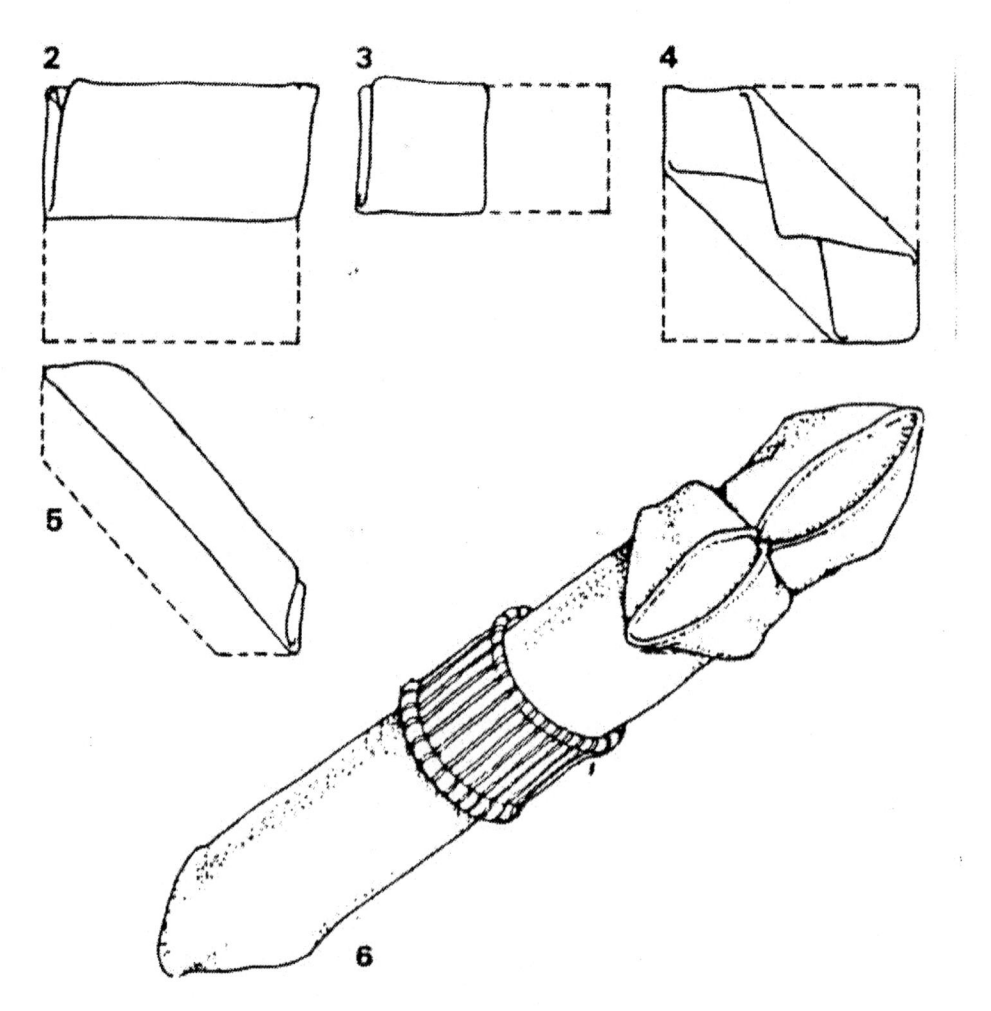

Napkin Folds

THE SWIRL

1. Lay the napkin out flat.
2. Starting with one of the corners, roll the napkin up.
3. Bend the napkin in the middle and place it in a glass.

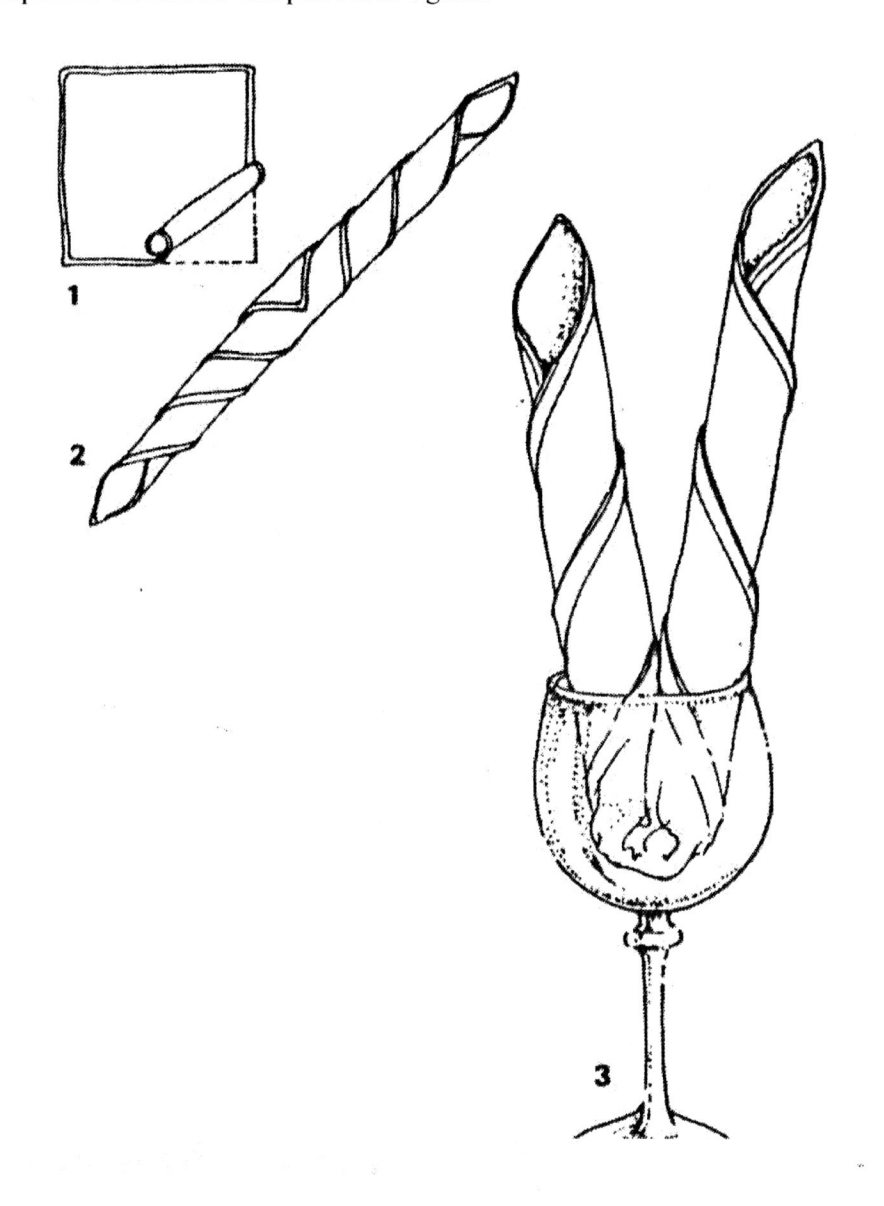

Informal Lunch

THE BOOK

1. Fold the napkin into thirds.
2. Fold the left and right sides over one quarter.
3. Fold both sides over again to meet in the center.
4. Fold the right side under the left.
5. Slide the napkin to make 3 equal folds.

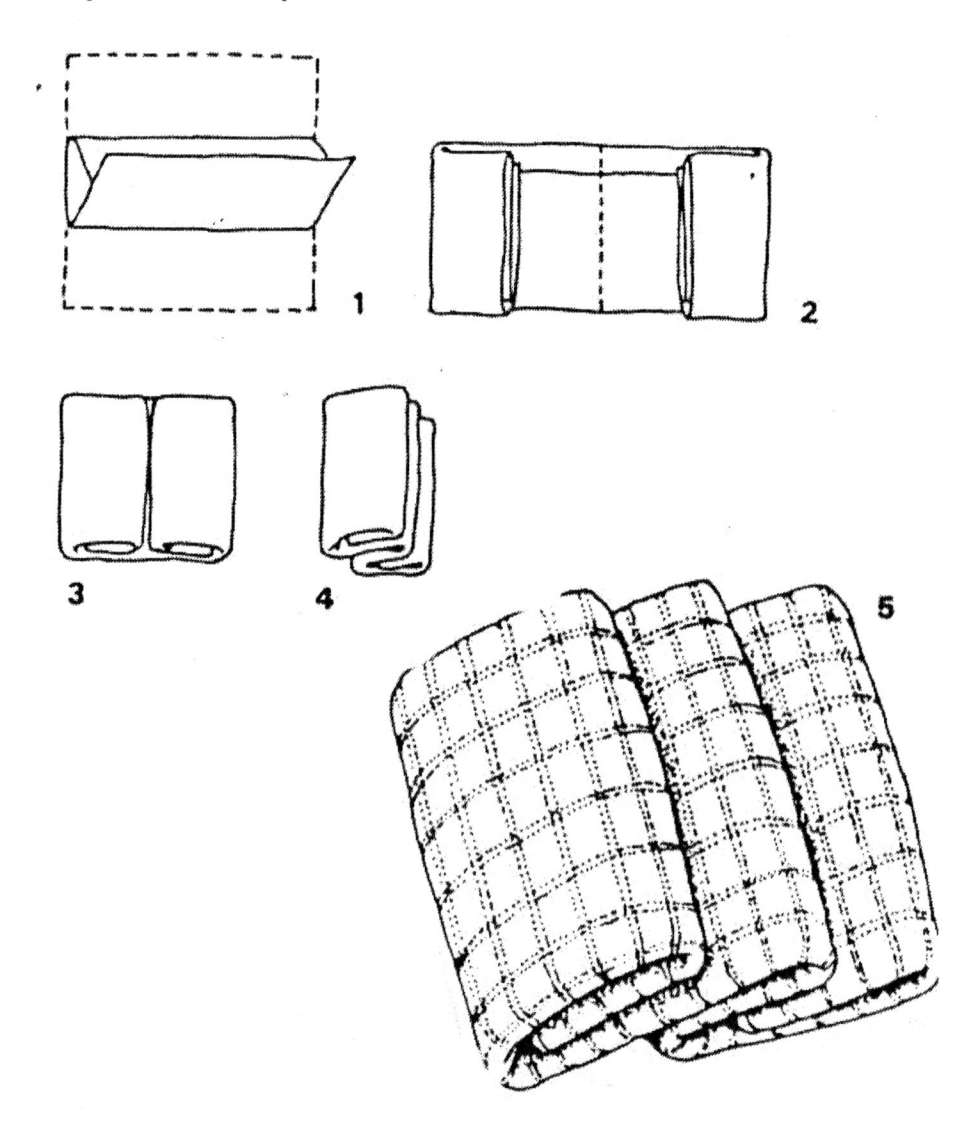

Birthday

THE LILY

1. Fold the napkin into quarters with the free corners at the top.
2. Fold the bottom corner to the center.
3. Fold the napkin in half.
4. Pleat each half.
5. Slip the bottom into a glass and open out the leaves.

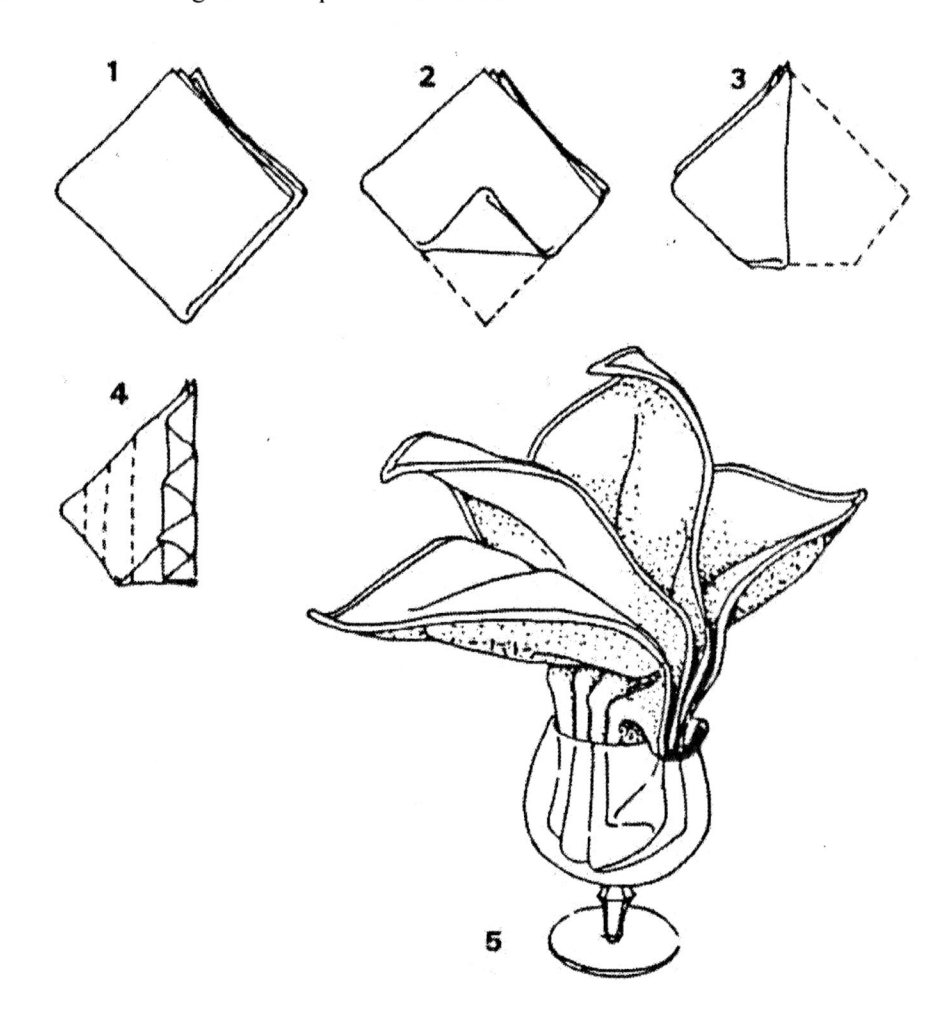

Midnight Supper

THE SAILBOAT

1. Fold the napkin in half diagonally.
2. Fold in half diagonally again.
3. Fold the bottom edge up by 1 inch twice.
4. Turn the napkin over, fold the flaps into each other and stand the napkin upright.

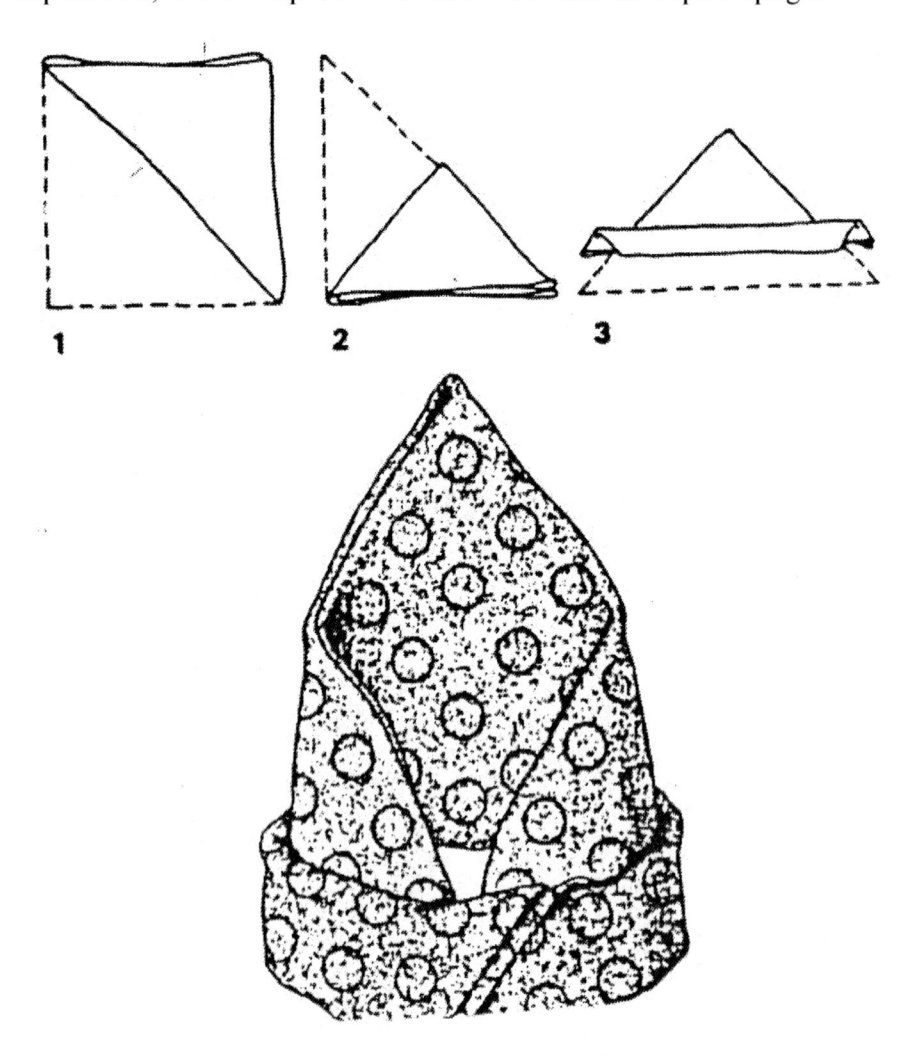

THE DOUBLE DIAMONDS

1. Fold the napkin into quarters with the free corners at the top.
2. Fold the first flap down to the bottom.
3. Fold the point back to the center of the napkin.
4. Fold the second flap down to the center.
5. Fold the sides of the napkin underneath.

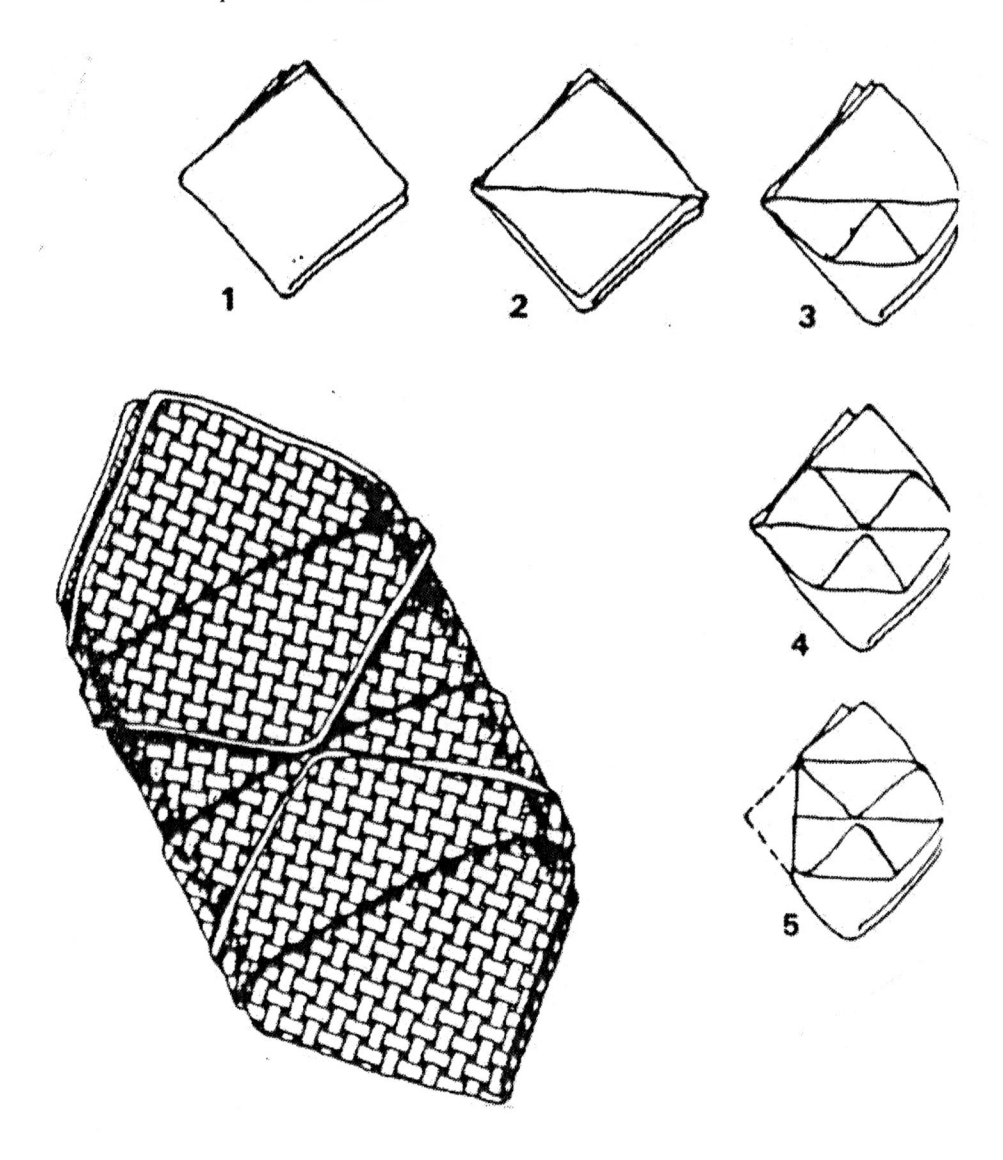

Children's Party

THE SURPRISE PACKAGE

1. Fold the napkin into quarters with the free corners at the top.
2. Fold the bottom and side corners to the center.
3. Turn the napkin over and fold the first flap down halfway.
4. Insert a surprise.

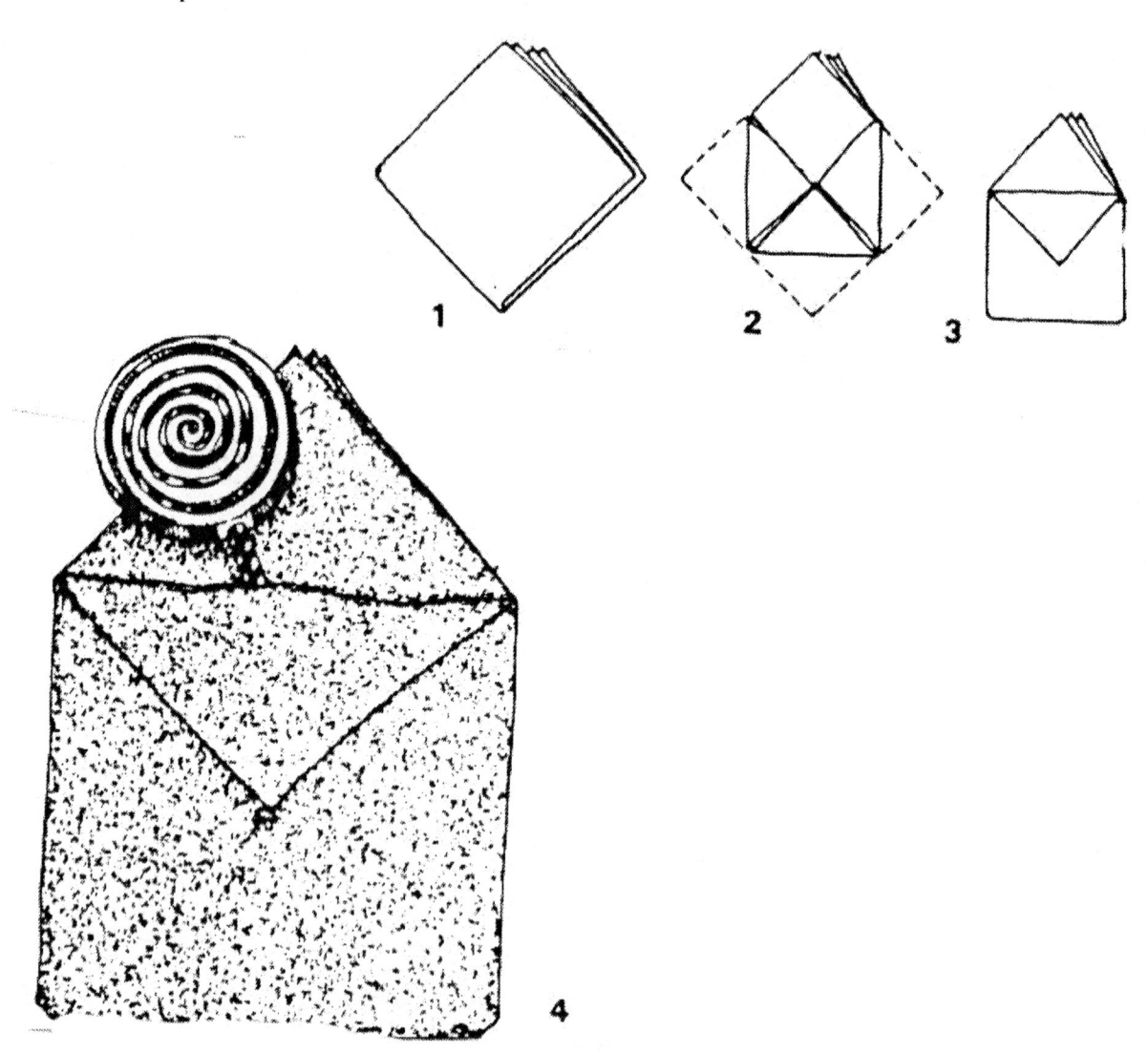

THE HAVANA

1. Fold the napkin into quarters with the free corners at the bottom.
2. Fold the top flap up one half.
3. Fold each of the remaining flaps up to within 1 inch of the previous flap.
4. Fold back the sides and lay the napkin flat.

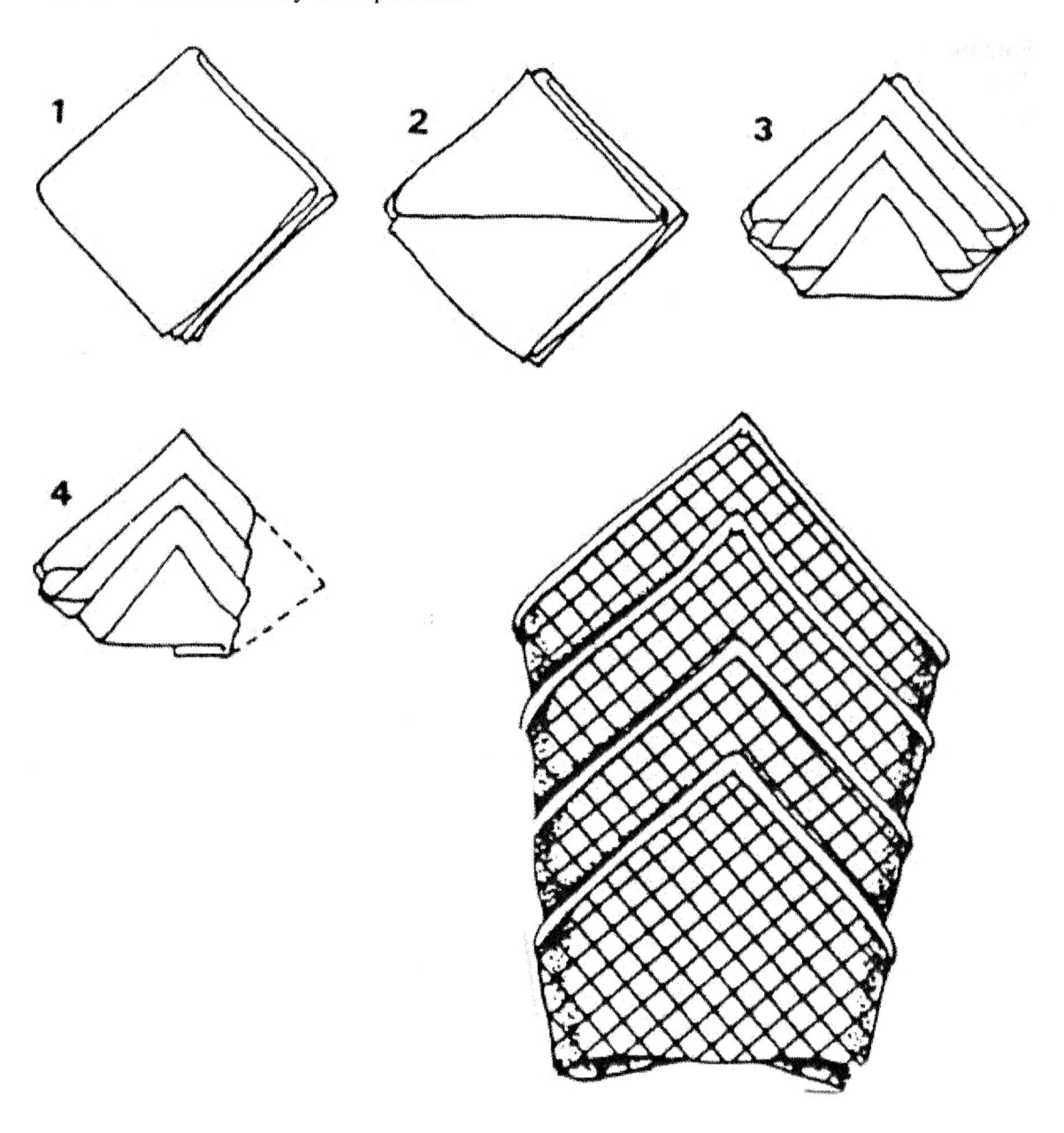

Barbecue

THE PYRAMID

1. Fold the napkin into quarters.
2. Fold it in half diagonally.
3. Bend the napkin in the middle and stand it upright.

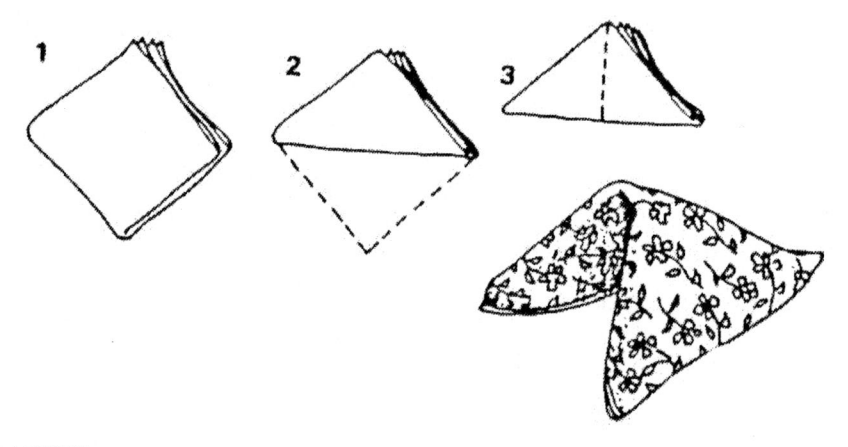

THE BONAPARTE

1. Fold the napkin in half diagonally.
2. Fold the bottom left and right corners to the top, forming a diamond.
3. Fold the bottom corner up, leaving about 1 inch at the top and lay the napkin flat.

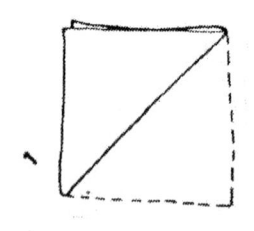

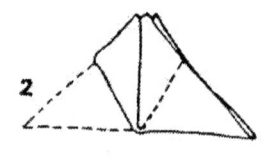

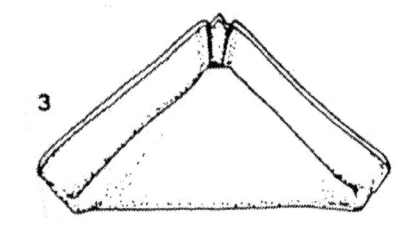

THE ASCOT TIE

1. Fold the napkin in half diagonally.
2. Fold the bottom edge up by one quarter twice.
3. Fold the sides over.
4. Turn the napkin over and lay it flat.

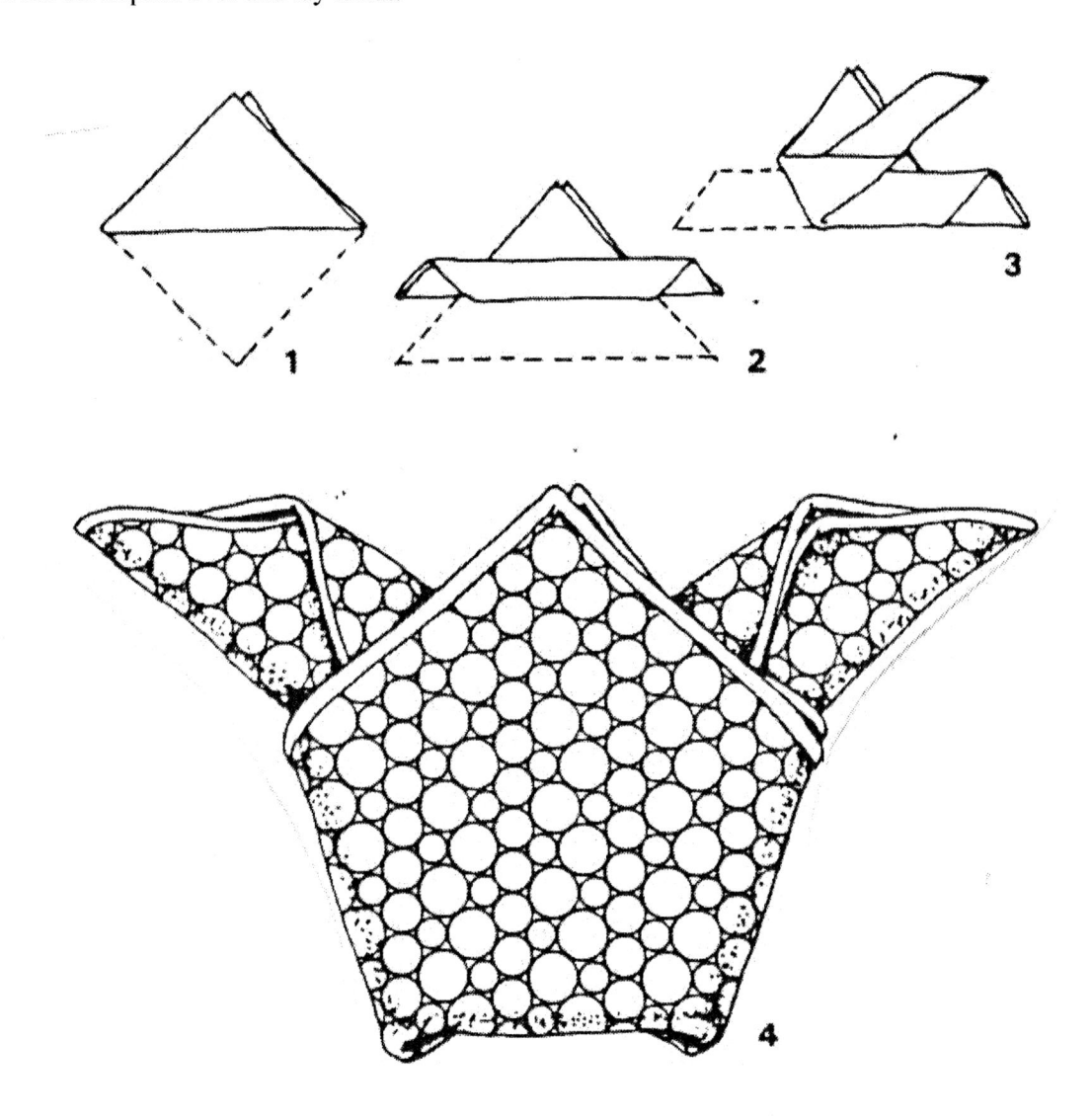

Afternoon Tea

A LA MAISON

1. Fold the napkin into quarters.
2. Turn up the bottom corner.
3. Fold into thirds.
4. Turn the napkin over and lay it flat.

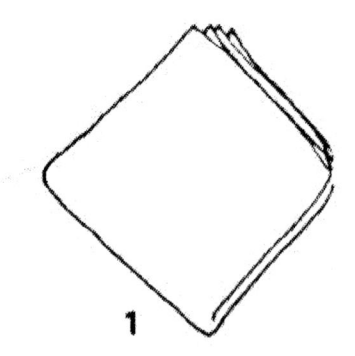

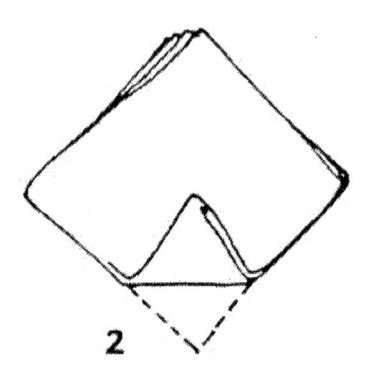

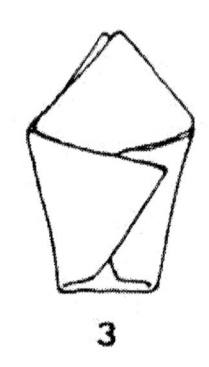

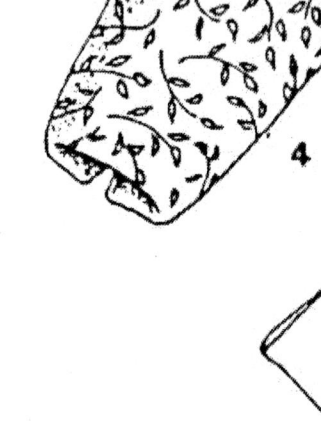

THE AMERICANA

1. Fold the napkin into quarters.
2. Fold the bottom and side corners to the center.
3. Fold into thirds.
4. Slip through a napkin ring.

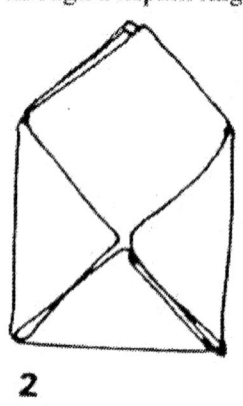

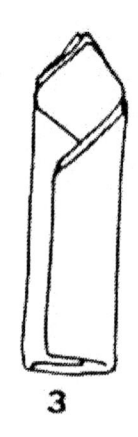

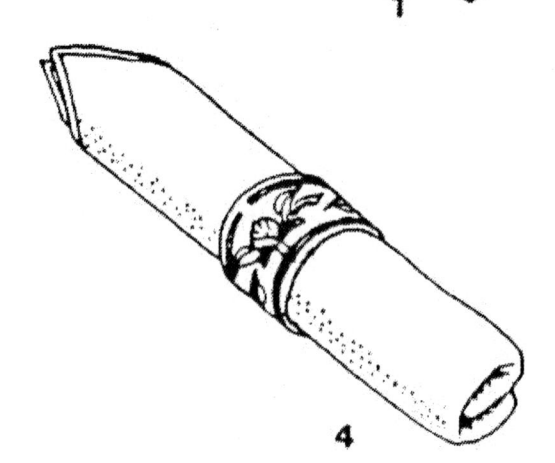

Buffet

THE BUFFET SERVER

8   Fold the napkin in half.
9   Fold the top flap back one half.
10 Turn the napkin over. Fold it into quarters and insert the utensils.

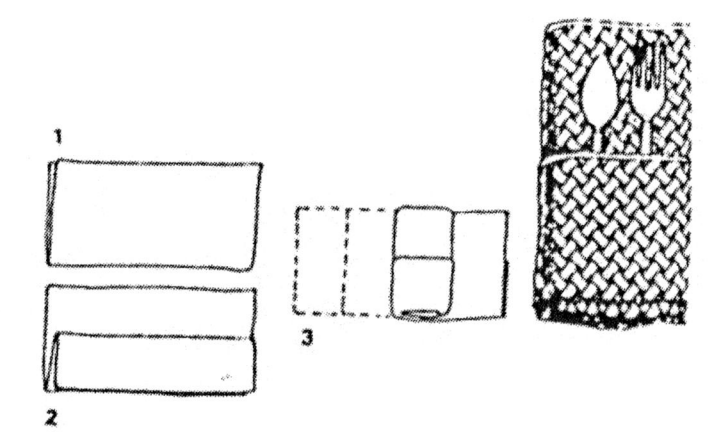

THE SPECIAL BUFFET SERVER

1   Fold each of the 4 corners to the center of the napkin.
2   Fold in half with the previous folds facing out.
3   Fold in half again.
4   Fold both sides underneath and insert the utensils.

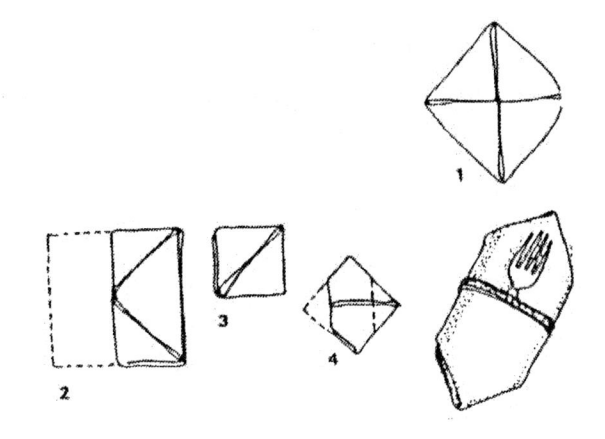

Breakfast in Bed

THE CANDLE

1. Fold the napkin in half diagonally.
2. Fold the bottom edge up about 1 inch.
3. Turn the napkin over and roll it up.
4. Tuck the end corner into the bottom of the roll and stand the napkin upright.

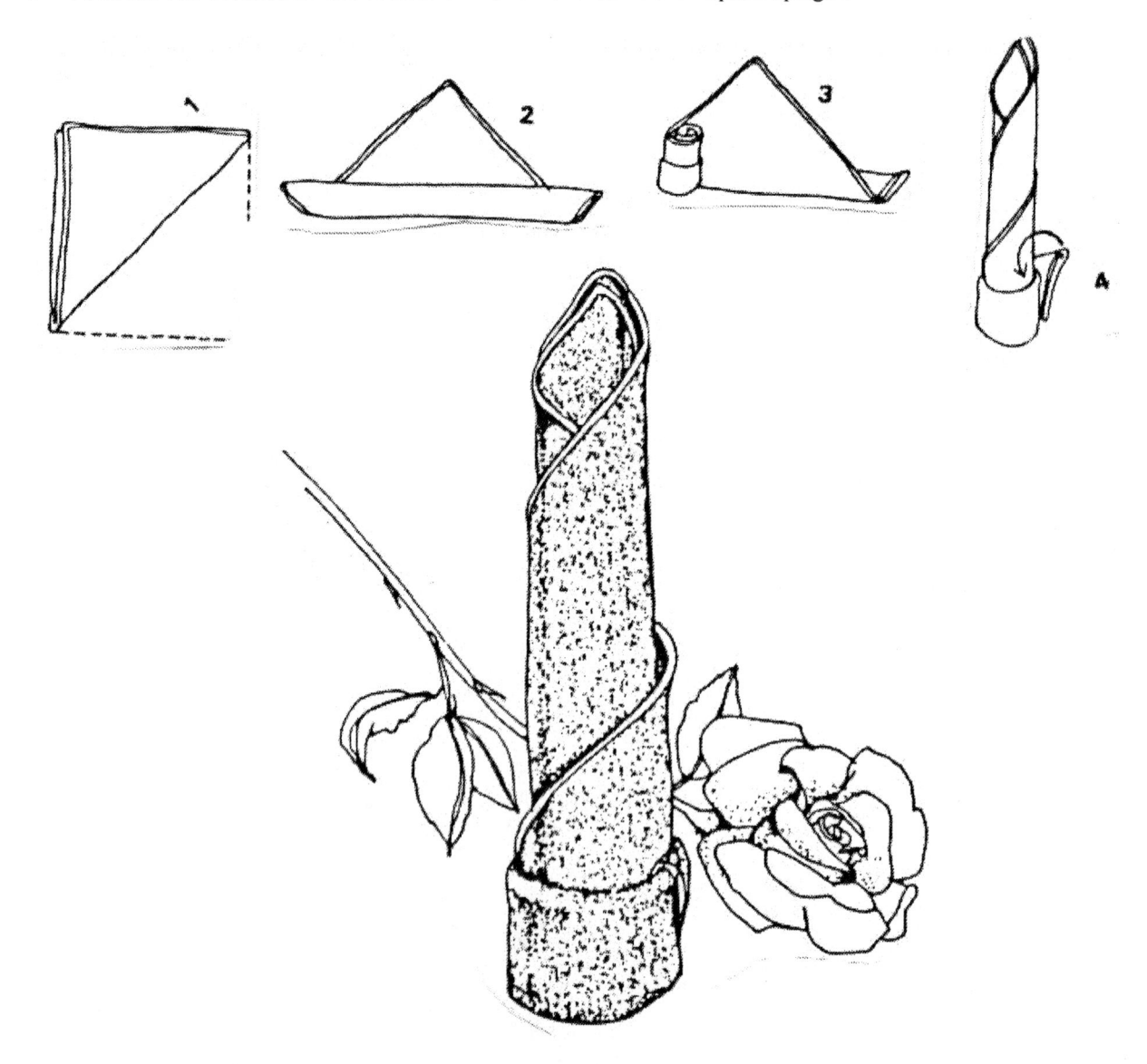

Holiday

THE STANDING FAN

1. Fold the napkin in half.
2. Pleat in 1-inch accordion pleats, leaving about 4 inches at the right.
3. Fold the napkin in half with the pleats facing out and with the bend on the bottom.
4. Fold the back down and tuck it behind the pleats. (This will form the stand.)
5. Stand the napkin up, allowing the pleats to form a fan.

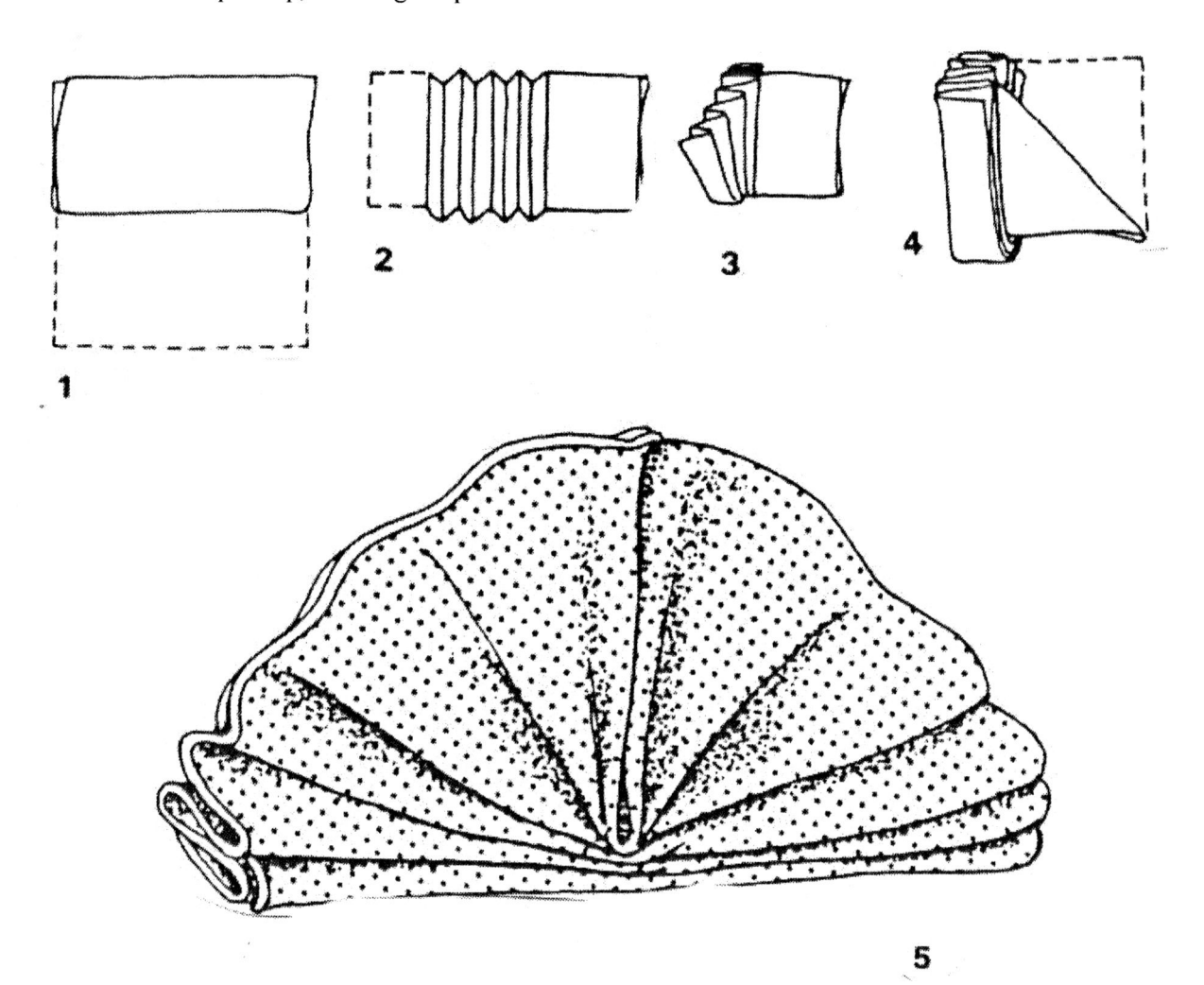

FLOWERS,

LEARN HOW TO MAKE FLOWER DESIGNS

VICTORIAN BOUQUET

Materials

- 3 Stems (pink) English garden "Dried Look" freesia
- 5 Stems (pink) romance rose
- 5 Stems (red) romance rose
- 1 Stem mini English ivy spray
- Preserved baby's breath
- Floral wire
- 1 1/2 yards (white) 1" french ribbon
- Potpourri oil

Tools

- Scissors
- Wire cutters
- Hot glue gun/glue sticks

Instructions

1. Cut freesia stems to 5" & 6" lengths. In your hand, surround one freesia stem with baby's breath.

2. Next, place one pink rose on left of freesia and one at the right. Place one red rose in front of freesia and one in back. Add more baby's breath. Continue this pattern until all roses have been added to bouquet.

3. Take remaining freesia stems and place one on left side and the other on the right. Add more baby's breath.

4. Cut stems from ivy leaves and hot glue leaves throughout bouquet and around edges of arrangement.

5. Wrap a piece of floral wire around stems of bouquet. Twist wire and cut. Cut stems to length of precut freesias so all stems are 5" – 6" long.

6. Wrap stems with 1-1/2 yards of white french ribbon. Start from bottom and wrap up stems. Tie a bow with remainder of ribbon around bottom of bouquet.

7. Add a few drops of potpourri oil on flowers for scent.

Field Flower Wreath

Materials

- 14" Grapevine wreath
- 2 Stems (purple) mini liatris
- 2 Stems (yellow) mini sunflower
- 2 Stems (pink) mini hydrangea
- 4 Stems "Feels Real" mini eucalyptus spray
- Spanish moss
- 1 Mushroom bird
- 4 Yards (pink) ribbon (1 1/2" width)
- Floral wire
- 4 Stems (fuchsia) mini rose spray
- 2 stems (yellow) mini field daisy spray
- 2 Stems (lavender) mini field daisy spray

Tools

- Hot glue gun/glue sticks
- Wire cutters
- Scissors

Instructions

1. Cut 3" off the bottom of all the stems (except for mini daisies and eucalyptus). Cut mini field daisy sprays in half to create eight bunches. Cut one eucalyptus spray in half and the remaining sprays in stems of various lengths between 4" and 8".

2. Hot glue a small amount of Spanish moss to upper right side of wreath. Hot glue bird on moss, small pieces of eucalyptus around bird and a bunch of yellow mini field daisies above the nest and below it.

3. Hot glue rest of Spanish moss on left side of wreath as shown.

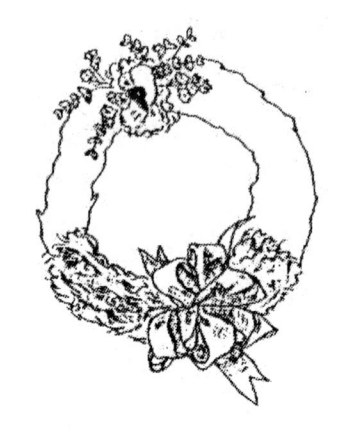

4. Create a large floral bow with 3 1/2" double pointed tails and attach to center left side of wreath with floral wire.

5. Divide remaining flowers and eucalyptus into two groups using equal amounts of styles and colors in each. Hot glue one group above the bow and the other below (see photo).

American Palette

Materials

- *13" x 5" x 4 1/2" Egg shaped bamboo basket*
- *Floral foam*
- *Spanish Moss*
- *Floral pins*
- *3 Stems (burgundy) peony*
- *2 Stems (rawhide) large tiger lily spray*
- *3 Stems (blue) Antique "Dried Look" rose*
- *3 Stems dusty miller spray*
- *3 Stems (rawhide) berry spray*
- *2 Yards (blue) "Paper Twirl" ribbon*

Tools

- *Scissors*
- *Wire cutters*
- *Hot glue gun/glue sticks*

Instructions

1. Hot glue floral foam to bottom of basket. Cover floral foam with moss and secure with floral pins.

2. Cut peony stems to 3"-5" lengths (save remaining stems). Insert one small bud in the center of the basket on the left side of the handle. Insert another small bud out the end on the left side. Arch the stems down. Place remaining peony blooms in front, back and center on the left side of the basket. (Tip: Always hot glue stem tips before inserting into floral foam.)

3. Cut tiger lily stems to 3"-5" lengths (save remaining stems) and insert tallest stem in place just above peonies. Place remaining lilies on each side and in the center.

4. Cut stems on roses to 4"-6" lengths (save remaining stems). Distribute throughout arrangement. Hot glue to secure. Cut berry sprays and dusty miller sprays into several pieces 4"-6" long and insert throughout arrangement filling in any empty spaces.

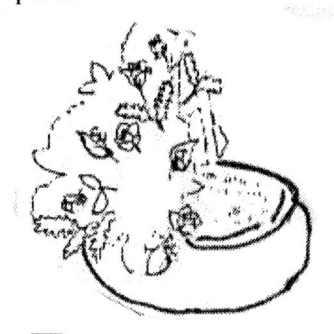

5. Hot glue stem tips and insert remaining stems at a horizontal angle into floral foam to extend out over the right side of basket. Use various stems to give the effect of flowers laying in a basket.

6. Make a four loop paper twirl bow with 9" tails. Hot glue on top of stems as shown.

ORIENTAL EXPRESSION

Materials

- *6" Flower pot with oriental design*
- *Floral foam*
- *5 Stems (mauve) peony*
- *2 Stems (pink) English garden "Dried Look" freesia*
- *2 Stems (rawhide) pixie rose spray*

Tools

- *Serrated knife*
- *Wire cutters*
- *Hot glue gun/glue sticks*

Instructions

1 Push floral foam into flower pot; it should fit snugly with 1/2" left above the rim. Hot glue to secure.

2 Cut peony stems to 5" lengths (save leaves). Hot glue stem tips and insert one in center with four evenly spaced around it. Cut leaves leaving 2"-3" stems and hot glue around flowers.

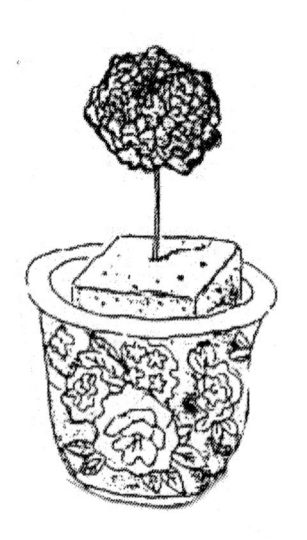

3 Cut freesia stems to 2"-3" lengths. Hot glue stem tips and insert freesia in between peonies.

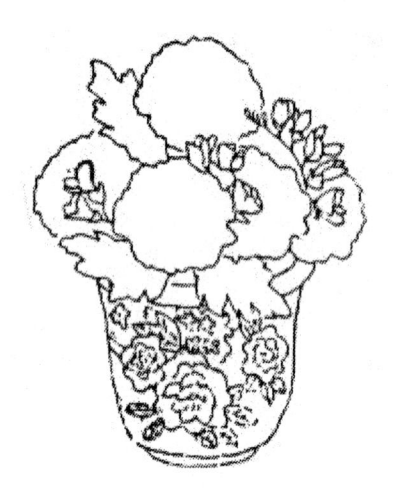

4 Cut each pixie rose spray into three stems 4"-5" long. Hot glue stem tips and insert into floral foam in-between peonies and freesia filling in any gaps.

NATURE'S WONDER

Materials

- *10" Grapevine wreath*
- *Spanish moss*
- *1 Stem "Feels Real" mini eucalyptus spray*
- *2 Stems (purple) mini field daisy spray*
- *1 Stem (white) mini baby's breath spray*
- *2 Stems (lavender) mini liatris*
- *4 Stems (melon) mini rose*
- *4 Stems (orange) mini mum*
- *1 Mushroom bird*

Tools

- *Hot glue gun/glue sticks*
- *Wire cutters*

Instructions

1. Spread Spanish moss over front of wreath. Cut eucalyptus into various lengths between 3" and 5". Attach both eucalyptus and Spanish moss with hot glue and distribute evenly to cover the entire wreath.

2. Cut apart the field daisy sprays, baby's breath and liatris into smaller sprays and pieces. Hot glue evenly spaced all around wreath.

3. Cut rose and mum stems to 1" in length. Hot glue mums and roses to wreath evenly spaced.

4. Hot glue bird to wreath, positioning as shown.

Dried Look Naturals

Materials

- 8" Oval natural basket with handle
- Floral foam
- Spanish moss
- Floral pins
- 3 Stems "Feels Real" purple passion foliage spray
- "Antique Dried Look" Stems:
- 11 Stems (mauve) rosebud
- 12 Stems (ivory) hydrangea
- 13 Stems (mauve) open rose
- 2 Stems (ivory) strawflower spray
- 14 Stems (ivory) baby's breath spray
- 15 Stems (mauve) sunflower spray

Tools

- Hot glue gun/glue sticks
- Wire cutters
- Scissors

Instructions

1. Hot glue bottom of floral foam and press firmly into basket. Cover floral foam with Spanish moss and secure in place with floral pins.

2. Trim 7" from the bottom of all three foliage sprays. Insert one in center, right and left. Spread leaves apart. (Tip: Always hot glue stem tips before inserting.)

3. Trim 2" from stems of rosebuds and insert as shown.

4. Cut hydrangea stems in half and place one at center front, one at center back and one extending out each side.

5. Cut the open rose stems in half and place three in the front and two in the back above hydrangea.

6. Trim 6" from one strawflower spray and place to the left of center. Trim 10" from remaining strawflower spray and place to the right of center (see photo).

7. Cut up baby's breath and sunflower sprays to desired lengths and place throughout for fullness.

FRESH PICKINGS

Materials

Fresh Pickings:
- Small watering can (approximately) 12" wide x 4" high)
- Floral foam
- Spanish moss
- 2 Deluxe mini foliage picks
- 2 Deluxe petite flower picks
- 3 Stems (fuchsia) English garden "Dried Look" sunflower spray

Boutique Hydrangea:
Small clay pot (2 1/2" diam.)
- Floral foam
- Spanish moss
- Floral pins
- 1 Stem (pink) English garden "Dried Look" large rosebud
- 1 Stem (pink) English garden "Dried Look" hydrangea
- 2/3 Yard (pink) wired ribbon (1" width)
- 2/3 Yard (lavender) wired ribbon (1" width)

For Double Hydrangea Style substitute:
- Small clay pot (4" diameter)
- 2 Stems (pink) English garden "Dried Look" hydrangea
- 1 Stem (white) Romance Rose
- 3/4 Yard (pink) wired ribbon (1" width)

Tools
- Serrated knife
- Wire cutters
- Hot glue gun/glue sticks

Instructions

1 *Fresh Pickings:*
Cut floral foam to fit snugly inside of watering can. Hot glue bottom of foam and press firmly into container. Cover floral foam with Spanish moss and hot glue in place.

2 Spread open foliage picks and insert on each side of can, allowing foliage to extend over container edge. (Tip: Hot glue stem tips before inserting.)

3 Spread apart petite flower picks and insert to the inside of where foliage was placed.

4 Trim stem of one sunflower spray to 15" and insert in center. Trim remaining sunflower stems to 11" and insert around the center flower.

Country Charm

Materials

- 9" Ceramic jug with stencil
- 3 Stems (eggplant) large tiger lily spray
- 2 Stems (blue) antique "Dried Look" Hydragea

Tools

- Wire cutters

Instructions

1. In your hand place two lily stems, staggering the heights so that one is lower than the other.

2. Under lower lily place one hydrangea stem. Add final lily stem facing out, in back of arrangement.

3. Add final hydrangea next to first hydrangea at the base of flowers.

4. Cut wire stems approximately 6"-7" below last flower and place entire arrangement into jug all at once.

FLORAL CANDLELIGHT

Materials

- *12" (Black) metal lantern*
- *Floral foam*
- *Spanish moss*
- *Mill moss (excelsior)*
- *Mushroom bird*
- *6 Stems "Feels Real" eucalyptus spray*
- *3 Stems (pink) English garden "Dried Look" rosebud spray*
- *3 Stems (pink) English garden "Dried Look" large open rose*
- *1 Stem (pink) English garden "Dried Look" large rosebud*
- *6 Stems (ivory) "Dried Look" baby's breath spray*
- *Handpainted butterfly*
- *Floral wire*

Tools

- *Serrated knife*
- *Wire cutters*
- *Hot glue gun/glue sticks*

Instructions

1. Cut floral foam to fit tightly in lantern. Carve a hole in the center for candle holder. Cover floral foam with Spanish moss and hot glue to secure.

2. Hot glue a small amount of mill moss to Spanish moss to make bird's nest. Hot glue nest to top edge of covered foam. Hot glue bird in nest.

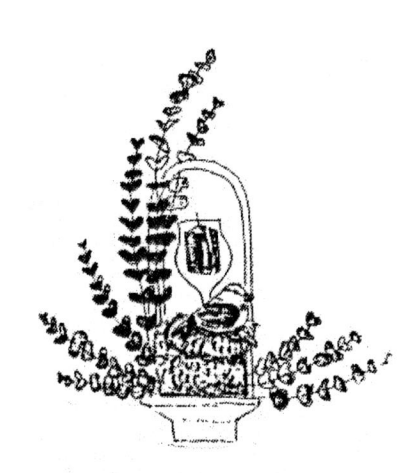

3. Cut three eucalyptus stems to 14", 16", and 18" lengths. Insert as shown into floral foam to give overall shape of arrangement. Cut apart three remaining eucalyptus sprays into stems varying between 6" to 10" and insert in all directions filling shape. (Tip: Hot glue stem tips before inserting in floral foam.)

4. Cut the length of one rosebud spray to 12" and insert alongside the tallest eucalyptus. Cut stems of three open roses to 8" and insert below tall rosebud spray. Cut large single rosebud stem to 12" and insert horizontally on right side. Cut remaining small rosebud sprays into separate stems of varying lengths and place throughout front and back of arrangement (see photo).

5. Trim baby's breath sprays into small bunches of 4" tall 7" lengths, hot glue in place to fill in gaps. Wire butterfly to the top of the lantern.

English Garden Windowbox

Materials

- *12" Oblong brass planter*
- *Floral foam*
- *Spanish moss*
- *3 Stems natural (yellow) sunflower*
- *2 Stems (pink) English garden "Dried Look" delphinium*
- *5 Stems (yellow/pink) English Garden "Dried Look" rose*
- *4 Stems (pink) English Garden "Dried Look" hydrangea*
- *2 Stems (green) onion grass spray*
- *3 Stems (chalk white) azara spray*
- *1 1/2 Yards (pink) wired ribbon (1 1/2" width)*
- *6 Foliage picks*
- *1 Small ivy bush*

Tools

- *Serrated knife*
- *Wire cutters*
- *Hot glue gun/glue sticks*
- *Scissors*

Instructions

1. Cut floral foam to fit snugly inside entire container and hot glue in place. Cover foam with Spanish moss and secure with hot glue.

2. Cut sunflower stems to 7", 12" and 15" lengths and insert on right. (Tip: Hot glue stem tips before inserting in floral foam.)

3. Cut delphinium stems to 10" and 14" lengths. Insert at angles on left side.

4. Cut rose stems to 3", 5", 8", and 2-7" lengths. Insert as shown.

5. Cut hydrangea stems to 6" and place throughout arrangement as shown.

6. Cut onion grass stems to 3" and insert behind sunflowers and hydrangeas on right.

7. Cut up azara sprays in varying lengths and place throughout arrangement. To fill in gaps, insert foliage picks near container edge underneath flowers.

8. Make a 5" loop bow with 8" tails and trim into a double pointed edge. Wire the center, attach to floral pick and insert in floral foam (see photo).

COTTAGE CLIPPINGS

Materials
- 18" Oval grapevine wreath
- 4" Clay pot
- Floral foam
- Spanish moss
- Floral moss
- 1 Stem variegated begonia foliage spray
- 1 Stem (fuchsia) beather
- 1 Stem (white) dogwood spray
- 1 Stem (yellow/pink) English garden "Dried Look" Prince rose
- Floral wire
- 1 Stem (fuchsia) pixie rose spray
- 1 Stem (rawbide) berry spray
- 1 Handpainted butterfly
- 1 Yard (print) ribbon (1" width)
- 2 Stems mini English ivy spray
  - *Tools*
- Pencil
- Small hammer
- Serrated knife
- Wire cutters
- Hot glue gun/glue sticks

1. To split pot in half, first draw a pencil line around pot. Holding pot upside down, tap gently (but with some force) with small hammer along line until pot splits in two. Edges will be uneven. Pick the best half to use for this project.

Instructions

2. Cut floral foam to fit snugly inside half pot, hot glue in place. Cover foam with Spanish moss, hot glue in place. Allow moss to spill out over top of pot. Generously apply hot glue to lower back portion of pot and firmly press to bottom of wreath until secure. Cover seams with Spanish moss and floral moss. Randomly hot glue Spanish moss around wreath.

3. Cut begonia foliage into three pieces between 5" and 8". Insert tallest piece at left side to curve up and shortest pieces at right to hang down over pot edge. Trim length of heather to 15", insert at center. (Tip: Always hot glue stem tips before inserting.)

4. Cut dogwood spray into four varying lengths between 5" and 9". Insert the two tallest pieces behind the heather. Insert remaining pieces at front right and front left.

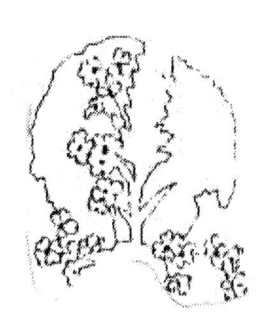

5. Cut Prince rose stem to 5" and insert in center front. Cut berry spray into five stems of varying lengths from 3" to 9" and insert as shown.

6. Cut pixie rose spray into four varying lengths between 5" and 9" and insert in floral foam to fill in empty spaces.

7. Make a 5" loop bow with 4" tails and attach with floral wire to bottom left side of wreath. Hot glue butterfly to upper right. Cut apart ivy sprays into stems of varying lengths between 4" and 6" and hot glue around outside perimeter of wreath.

Botanical Sculpture

Materials
- *5" Clay flower pot saucer*
- *Floral foam*
- *Spanish moss*
- *Floral pins*
- *4 Stems (orange) large gladiola*
- *2 Stems (ivory) camellia spray*
- *3 Stems curly willow branch*

Tools

- *Hot glue gun/glue sticks*
- *Wire cutters*

Instructions

1 Place floral foam in saucer and secure with hot glue. Cover with moss and secure with floral pins.

2 Hot glue stem tip and insert one gladiola into the floral foam in back. Cut remaining gladiolas, 2"-4" shorter (staggering heights) and insert downward towards the front. Hot glue stem tips to secure.

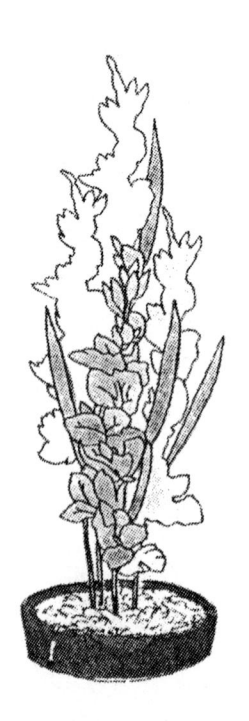

3 Cut apart the camellia sprays into stems of 4"-7". Place in front. Stagger the heights and cover the foam. Hot glue stem tips to secure.

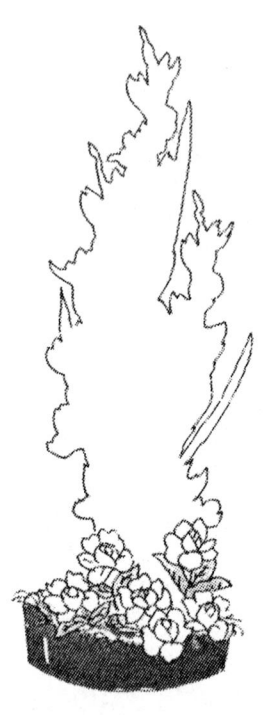

4 Add curly willow branches to the left side and back as shown in photograph. Hot glue in place.

GOOD BEHAVIOR: GOOD BEHAVIOR: GOOD BEHAVIOR

CLEAN HANDS — DIRTY HANDS SPREAD GERMS, HANDS AND FINGERNAILS SHOULD BE WASHED VERY THOROUGHLY WITH SOAP AND WATER BEFORE YOU EAT, AFTER USING THE TOILET AND EVERY TIME THEY ARE SOILED.

HOW TO WASH YOUR HANDS

MAKE SURE THAT YOU WASH YOUR HANDS ALL THE TIME TO KEEP THEM CLEAN ALWAYS.

WET YOUR HANDS WITH WATER.

APPLY SOAP WASH UNDER NAILS AND BETWEEN FINGERNAILS.

RUB HANDS TOGETHER FOR A FEW MINUTES TRY TO MAKE SURE THAT THEY ARE CLEAN MAKE ROTATING MOVES. WASH YOUR WRIST AS WELL.

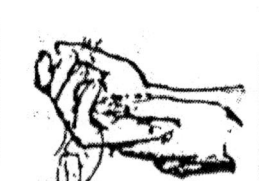

WASH FINGERS AND SPACES BETWEEN FINGERS.

RINSE HANDS VERY WELL.

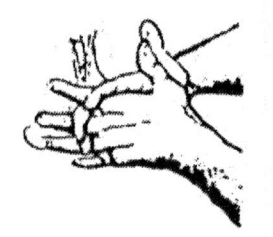

DRY HANDS WITH TOWEL.

GERMS

IT IS VERY IMPORTANT THAT FOOD IS SAFE TO EAT: IF FOOD IS NOT SAFE TO EAT YOU CAN GET SICK FROM BAD FOOD.

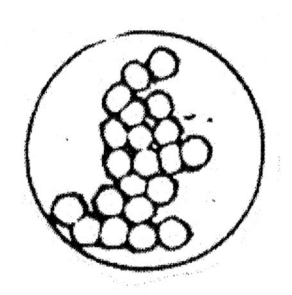

STAPHYLOCOCCUS AUREUS

(STAPHYLOCOCCAL FOOD POISONING)

YOU CAN GET SICK FROM THIS TYPE OF GERM

GERMS

    IT IS VERY IMPORTANT THAT FOOD IS SAFE TO EAT: IF FOOD IS NOT SAFE TO EAT YOU CAN GET SICK FROM BAD FOOD.

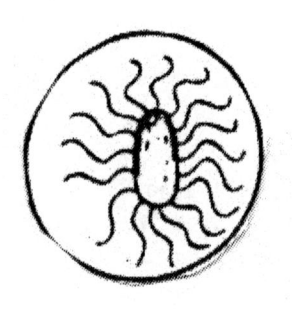

SALMONELLA
(SALMONELLOSIS)

YOU CAN GET SICK FROM THIS TYPE OF GERM

GERMS

IT IS VERY IMPORTANT THAT FOOD IS SAFE TO EAT: If FOOD IS NOT SAFE TO EAT YOU CAN GET SICK FROM BAD FOOD.

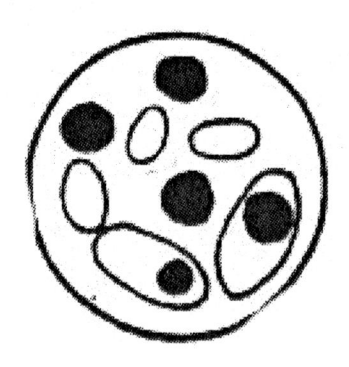

CLOSTRIDIUM PERFRINGENS
(CLOSTRIDIUM PERFRINGENS GASTROENTERITIS)

YOU CAN GET SICK FROM THIS TYPE OF GERM

COOK IT!

Cooking kills harmful bacteria. Be sure ground meat and ground poultry are cooked thoroughly.

Cook it safely

- The center of patties and meat loaf should not be pink and the juices should run clear.
- Crumbled ground meats should be cooked until no pink color remains.
- Ground meat patties and loaves are safe when they reach 160° F in the center; ground poultry patties and loaves, 165°F.

Cook it evenly

- During broiling, grilling, or cooking on the stove, turn meats over at least once.
- When baking, set oven no lower than 325° F.
- If microwaving, cover meats. Midway through cooking, turn patties over and rotate the dish; rotate a meat loaf; and stir ground meats once or twice. Let microwaved meats stand to complete cooking process.

After cooking, refrigerate leftovers immediately. Separate into small portions for last cooling.

To reheat all leftovers, cover and heat to 165° or until hot and steaming throughout.

CLEAN IT!

Keep EVERYTHING clean—hands, utensils, counters, cutting boards and sinks. That way, your food will stay as safe as possible.

- Always wash hands thoroughly in hot soap and water before preparing foods and after handling raw meat.
- Don't let raw meat or poultry juices touch ready-to-eat foods either in the refrigerator or during preparation.
- Don't put cooked foods on the same plate that held raw meat or poultry.
- Wash utensils that have touched raw meat with hot, soap and water before using them for cooked meals.
- Wash counters, cutting boards and other surfaces raw meats have touched. And don't forget to keep the inside of your refrigerator clean.

VITAMINS ARE GOOD TO LEARN ABOUT

Vitamins

Vitamins	Functions in the Body	Some Good Food Sources
Thiamin (B-1)	Helps the body use the energy from carbohydrates. Needed for normal functioning of the nervous system.	Whole-grain breads and cereals, pork, liver, melons, oranges, peas, sunflower seeds
Riboflavin (B-2)	Helps the body obtain energy from carbohydrates, fats, and proteins.	Whole-grain breads and cereals, broccoli, spinach, sweet potatoes, beef, chicken, liver, milk, cheese, yogurt
Niacin (B-3)	Helps the body obtain energy from carbohydrates, fats, and proteins.	Whole-grain breads and cereals, mushrooms, potatoes, chicken, Cornish hens, lamb, liver, veal, mackerel, salmon, swordfish, tuna
B-6	Helps the body use proteins to build tissue. Aids in the burning of fat for energy.	Fortified cereals, bananas, plantain, chicken, liver, spinach
B-12	Used in the formation of red blood cells. Helps the nervous system to function.	Beef, lamb, crabmeat, pork, eggs, clams, oysters, salmon, trout, tuna
Folic acid	Aids in the formation of red blood cells. Helps to build structures in every cell in the body.	Fortified cereals, black-eyed peas, spinach, liver, red kidney beans, lentils

MINERALS ARE GOOD TO LEARN ABOUT

Minerals

Mineral	Functions in the body	Some Good Food Sources
Calcium	Used to build and maintain strong bones and teeth. Helps muscles to contract and blood to clot. Maintains cell membranes.	Milk, cheese, yogurt, broccoli, turnip greens, sardines, tofu (bean curd), canned salmon (with bones), dark green leafy vegetables
Iron	As part of hemoglobin in the blood, iron carries oxygen to all of the cells in the body.	Fortified cereals, lima beans, spinach, beef, liver, clams, oysters, black-eyed peas, chick peas (garbanzos)
Magnesium	Used to build bones, make proteins from amino acids, regulate body temperature, and obtain the energy stored in muscles as glycogen.	Whole-grain breads and cereals, artichokes, lima beans, broccoli, okra, spinach, tofu, black-eyed peas, chick peas
Copper	Helps to maintain bones, blood vessels, and nerves. Needed to form hemoglobin in the blood.	Barley, whole-wheat bread, prunes, potatoes in their skins, turnip greens, mushrooms, liver, lobster, oysters, nuts and seeds
Zinc	Aids in healing wounds, forming blood cells, and growing and maintaining all body tissues.	Beef, lamb, chicken, liver, oysters, yogurt, eggs, fortified cereals
Phosphorus	Helps to form bones and teeth, cell membranes, and enzymes. Plays a role in releasing energy from carbohydrates, fats, and proteins.	Whole-grain breads and cereals, beef, chicken, lamb, liver, pork, catfish, mackerel, salmon, swordfish, lima beans, eggs, milk
Potassium	Aids in muscle contraction. Maintains the chemical balance in cells. Transmits nerve impulses. Helps to get energy from carbohydrates, fats and proteins.	Apricots, bananas, orange juice, milk, yogurt, peaches, pomegranates, prunes, lima beans, Swiss chard, plantain, potatoes, winter squash, sweet potatoes, tomatoes, lentils, peas
Iodine	Used to form hormones in the thyroid gland. Needed for normal reproduction.	Seafood, seaweed, iodized salt, sea salt

AMINO ACIDS

- It is very important to learn about amino acids.
- Each amino acid contain carbon hydrogen and nitrogen.
- Cysteine and Methionine contain sulfur.
- Carbohydrates and Fats are food chemicals that contain hydrogen and oxygen.
- All Amino Acids have a Acid Group made from Carbon, Hydrogen, and Oxygen Atoms.

AMINO ACIDS ARE GOOD TO LEARN ABOUT

These are the 20 amino acids in human proteins			
Alanine	(A)	*Leucine	(L)
Arginine	(R)	*Lysine	(K)
Asparagine	(N)	*Methionine	(M)
Aspartic acid	(D)	*Phenylalanine	(F)
Cysteine	(C)	Proline	(P)
Glutamic acid	(E)	Serine	(S)
Glutamine	(O)	*Threonine	(T)
Glycine	(G)	*Tryptophan	(W)
*Histidine	(H)	Tyrosine	(Y)
*Isoleucine	(I)	*Valine	(V)

LEARN ABOUT HERBS

ALFALFA
Alfalfa is a good source of carotene (Vitamin A). It is useful in reducing fevers. Alfalfa is very beneficial to the blood, acting as a blood purifier. Contains natural fluoride helping to prevent tooth decay.

ALOE
One of the great healing agents we have among the herbs. Works wonderfully in cleaning out the colon. Gives regular bowel movement. Aloe works well on any kind of sore on the outside of the body. Excellent remedy for piles and hemorrhoids.

ASTRAGALUS
This herb is an excellent energizer. It has been used by athletes for energy reserves, especially in the arms and legs. Also useful in cold climates for keeping the body warm. Used with Ginseng, it works as a total body energizer both inside and out. Astragalus will make a difference in your life. Try it!

BEE POLLEN
There are 22 basic elements in the human body – enzymes, hormones, vitamins, amino acids and others, which must be renewed by nutrient intake. No one food contains all of them…except Bee Pollen. The healing, rejuvenating and disease fighting effects of this total nutrient are hard to believe, yet are fully documented. Aging, digestive upsets, prostate diseases, sore throats, acne, fatigue, sexual problems, allergies and a host of other conditions have been successfully treated by the use of Bee Pollen. Vigorous good health has been maintained by the millions of people who make Bee Pollen a staple of their diets.

BILBERRY LEAF
Billberry strengthens tiny capillaries that feed eye muscles and nerves reducing and even reversing the damage caused by blood vessel deterioration. Increases night vision, reduces eye fatigue.

BLACK COHOSH
This is an excellent herb to regulate menstrual flow and for menstrual cramps. Black Cohosh has the same effects on the female system as synthetic estrogen, without the side effects. Best of all, Black Cohosh has no cancer causing agents like synthetic estrogen.

BLESSED THISTLE (Holy Thistle)
Blessed Thistle. Thistle is an excellent stimulant tonic for the stomach and heart. It aids circulation and helps to resolve liver problems. It takes oxygen to the brain and strengthens memory.

BROMELAIN
This fat melting enzyme works wonders. Bromelain flushes the fat from your body by naturally stimulating your metabolism and ridding your body of excess fluids.

BURDOCK LEAF & ROOT
Extremely good for removing toxins from the body. Strong blood purifier and cleanser. One of the best herbs for severe skin problems. Good for advanced cases of arthritis.

CAPSICUM (Cayenne)
One of the most important herbs. Not enough can be said about this wonderful healer. Normalizes blood pressure. Improves entire circulatory system. Feeds the cell structure of arteries, veins and capillaries so they will regain elasticity.

Capsicum is one of the best stimulants. When the body is stimulated properly, the healing and cleansing process starts, allowing the body to function normally. Stops bleeding on contact. Every home should have Capsicum on hand.

CHICKWEED
Rich in vitamin C and minerals – especially calcium, magnesium and potassium. This herb helps to carry toxins from the body. It will heal and soothe anything it comes in contact with. Dissolves plaque in blood vessels.

COLTSFOOT HERB & FLOWER
It is very soothing to the mucus membranes. Improves lung troubles. Excellent in relieving the chest of phlegm. Useful for asthma, bronchitis and spasmodic coughs.

CORNSILK
Useful for trouble with the prostate gland. Excellent remedy for kidney and bladder trouble.

CRANBERRY
Keeps your kidneys clean. Taken at the first sign of bladder or kidney infection (painful urination, back pain), Cranberry can often provide relief overnight. Each capsule contains 140mg Cranberry Juice Concentrate,

DANDELION LEAF & ROOT
The greatest benefit of this herb is to help detoxify any poisons in the liver. Dandelion has also been beneficial in lowering blood pressure.

DONG QUAI ROOT
This is a most wonderful herb for female troubles. It can help decrease the discomfort of menopause and post-menopause. It is rich in vitamins B-12 and E.

ECHINACEA ROOT
Works especially well in glandular infections and ailments. Used to treat strep throat, lymph glands. Cleanses the morbid matter from the stomach. Also expels poisons and toxins.

FENNEL SEED
Fennel is one of the most highly recommended remedies for gas, acid stomach, gout, cramps and spasms. Other benefits include: excellent obesity fighter, makes a good eyewash, and a good liver cleanser.

FENUGREEK SEED
Has been used in the following with excellent results: allergies, coughs, digestion, emphysema, headaches, migraines, intestinal inflammation, ulcers, lungs, mucous membranes, and sore throat.

FEVERFEW HERB
Anyone who suffers from migraines should give this herb a try. It works wonders in fighting against migraines. Thousands have successfully been helped without any side effects. Other benefits of this herb are: helps reduce inflammation in arthritic joints and has been used to restore the liver to normal function.

GINGER ROOT
It's a familiar spice, but few realize it can make us healthier. Here are a few things ginger is known for stimulating the circulatory system, a very good remedy for a sore throat, has a cleansing effect on the kidneys and bowels and helps prevent motion sickness.

GINKGO BILOBA
Ginkgo has been studied worldwide over the past two decades and scientific data concludes that Ginkgo can support the entire vascular system and so enhance circulation. In addition, reports validate Ginkgo's ability

to promote increased blood and oxygen flow to the brain which allows proper mental function. In Europe alone, over 20 million people take Ginkgo Biloba to feel their best...full of vitality and mentally alert.

GINSENG ROOT, SIBERIAN
This is a tremendously valuable herb. The Chinese call Ginseng a cure-all. Excellent to build resistance against stress, both mental and physical. Has been considered by many people to slow the aging process.

GOLDENSEAL
This herb is most valuable because it is a remedy for scores of ailments. Here are just a few examples: Bladder infections, bronchitis, cankers, coughs, colds, earaches, inflammations, mouth sores, mucous membranes, nasal passages, ulcers, and the list goes on. This is an expensive herb, but ask anyone that has ever used Goldenseal and they will tell you it's well worth it.

GOTA KOLA
Gota Kola is known as the "memory herb". It stimulates circulation to the brain. It's considered to be one of the best nerve tonics. Many people use Gota Kola to increase learning ability.

GREEN BARLEY
Extremely nutritious and an excellent antioxidant. Considered by many to help anything in the body that needs help. Twice the fiber of Oat Bran and 12 times more chlorophyll.

HAWTHORN
Hawthorn is highly regarded for its benefit to the heart. It is used to strengthen and regulate the heart. Good for people under stress. Useful in treating high and low blood pressure. Very effective in relieving insomnia.

HOPS FLOWER
Valuable for those with insomnia. Will produce sleep when nothing else will. Has been used successfully to decrease the desire for alcohol. Will tone liver.

HORSETAIL (Shavegrass)
Horsetail is rich in minerals, especially silica. Therefore it makes for strong fingernails and hair, good for split ends. Studies have shown that fractured bones will heal much faster when horsetail is taken. Good for eyes, ears, nose, throat, and glandular disorders.

HO SHOU WU
Excellent rejuvenator. Strengthens liver and kidneys.

SEAWRACK (Bladderwrack)
One of the best herbs to combat obesity. It has splendid effect on glandular afflictions. If one has been overweight for a long period of time without success in keeping the weight off, satisfying results are found with Seawrack.

SLIPPERY ELM BARK
Here's one of those herbs that works well for many ailments. Slippery Elm Bark has been used to normalize bowel movement and has been used beneficially to treat hemorrhoids and constipation. Helps to cleanse the colon, aids digestion and is a useful remedy for diarrhea, kidney troubles, and lung pain. Also eases eye pain.

SPIKENARD
Excellent herb for skin ailments such as acne, pimples, blackheads, rashes and general skin problems. Very useful in coughs, colds and all chest afflictions.

ST. JOHN'S WORT
Powerful as a blood purifier. Very good in cases of tumors and boils. Very good in

chronic uterine problems. Can help correct irregular menstruation.

THYME
Removes mucus from the head, lungs and respiratory passages. It's great for fighting infection. Also brings relief to migraines.

VALERIAN ROOT
Valerian is a wonderful gift from God. It has a most useful healing effect on the nervous system. Very quieting and calming. Good for entire circulatory system. Acts as a mild sedative and may promote sleep if taken as a tea at night.
NOTE: NEVER BOIL VALERIAN ROOT!

VERVAIN*
This herb should be in every home. A marvelous remedy for fevers. Will often clear a cold overnight. Good for expelling phlegm from throat and chest. Will expel worms when everything else fails. Excellent for shortness of breath and wheezing.

WILD YAM ROOT
Very relaxing and soothing to the nerves. For people who get excited easily, Wild Yam is most useful. It will also help expel gas from the stomach and bowels.

YELLOW DOCK ROOT
Most wonderful blood purifier, therefore good in all skin problems. Helps tone entire system.

YOHIMBE
Many believe that Yohimbe acts as a natural aphrodisiac for both men and women.

YUCCA ROOT
Reduces inflammation of the joints, therefore helpful for arthritic and rheumatoid problems. Makes an excellent hair and scalp treatment.

USE THE ALPHABET TO LEARN THE BODY

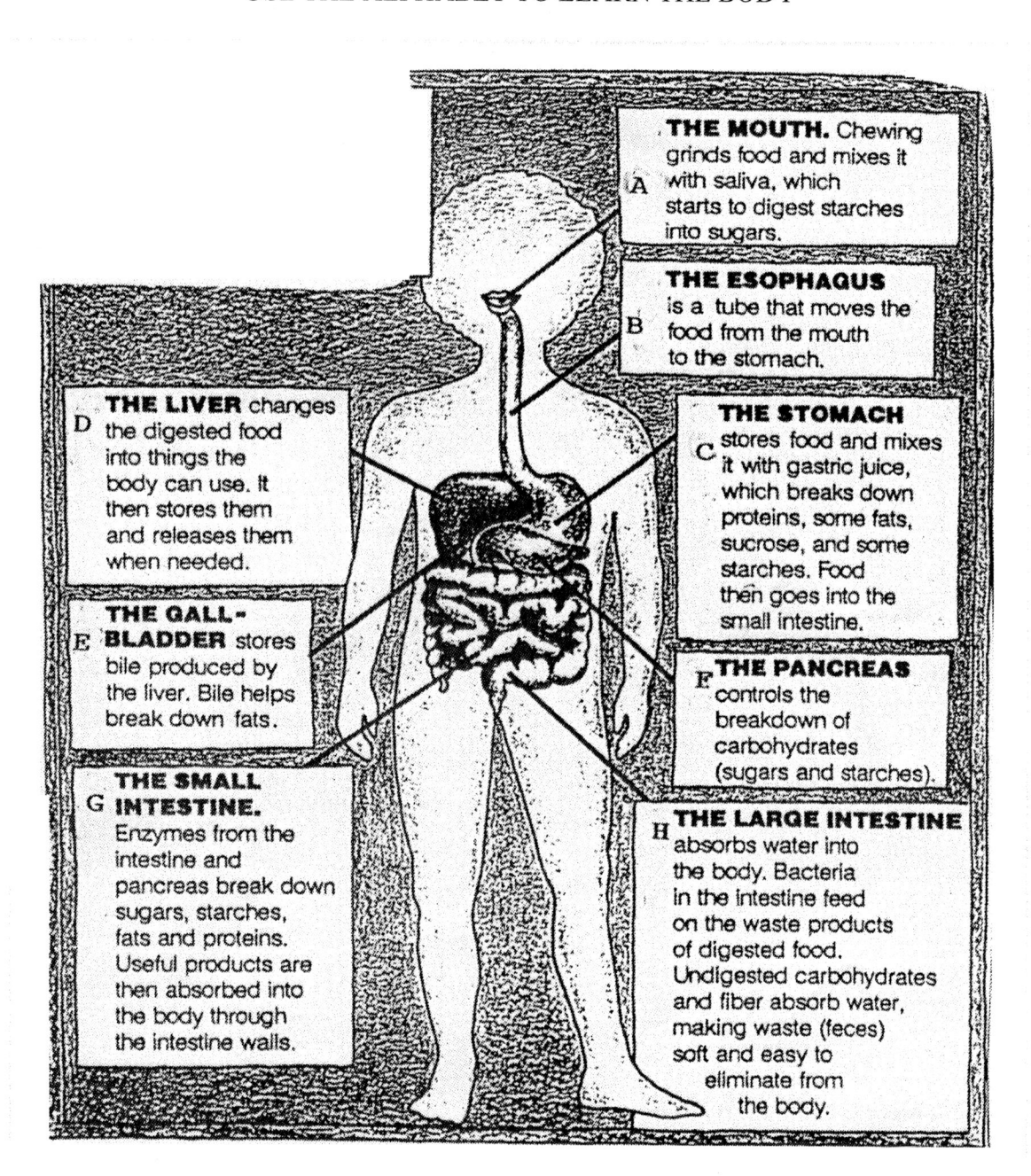

A — THE MOUTH. Chewing grinds food and mixes it with saliva, which starts to digest starches into sugars.

B — THE ESOPHAGUS is a tube that moves the food from the mouth to the stomach.

C — THE STOMACH stores food and mixes it with gastric juice, which breaks down proteins, some fats, sucrose, and some starches. Food then goes into the small intestine.

D — THE LIVER changes the digested food into things the body can use. It then stores them and releases them when needed.

E — THE GALL-BLADDER stores bile produced by the liver. Bile helps break down fats.

F — THE PANCREAS controls the breakdown of carbohydrates (sugars and starches).

G — THE SMALL INTESTINE. Enzymes from the intestine and pancreas break down sugars, starches, fats and proteins. Useful products are then absorbed into the body through the intestine walls.

H — THE LARGE INTESTINE absorbs water into the body. Bacteria in the intestine feed on the waste products of digested food. Undigested carbohydrates and fiber absorb water, making waste (feces) soft and easy to eliminate from the body.

GOOD HEALTHY FOODS TO EAT

The Meat and Milk Groups

The Meat Group

Beef	Fish and Shellfish
Lamb	Eggs
Chicken	Pork
Turkey	Peanut Butter
Dried Beans, Peas and Nuts	Soybeans
Seeds	Tofu

Eat two 2-3 oz. servings daily.

The Milk Group

Whole Milk	Dried Milk
Skim and Lowfat Milk	Ice Cream
Cheese (hard and soft)	Cottage Cheese
Evaporated Milk	Yogurt
Condensed Milk	

You need about four 8 oz. servings of milk daily.

GOOD HEALTHY FOODS TO EAT

The Bread and Cereal Group	**Flour and Grains**
Breads (white, wheat, rye, etc.)	Pasta
Rolls and Buns	Rice
Crackers and Biscuits	
Breakfast Cereals	

Eat four servings daily.
One serving equals one-half cup of cereal or one slice of bread.

GOOD HEALTHY FOODS TO EAT

The Vegetable and Fruit Group

Potatoes (white and sweet)	Apples
Corn	Grapes
Carrots	Tomatoes
Eggplant	Peaches
Cucumbers	Pears
Onions (all types)	Bananas
Celery	Pineapples
Beets	Pumpkins
Asparagus	Squash
Lettuce	Spinach

Eat four one-half cup servings daily.

HEALTH AND NUTRITION

NUTRITION TIPS

Most fruit provide vitamins, but some stand head and shoulders above the rest. Citrus fruit, berries, guava, kiwi fruit and pawpaw are the fruit richest in vitamin C, and worth eating on a daily basis. Orange-colored fruit like apricots, mangoes, and honeydew are rich in beta-carotene (the precursor of vitamin A).

♦ If the children refuse to eat vegetables, remember that fruit is the ideal substitute. Fruit supplies the same nutrients as vegetables, notably vitamins A and C, fiber and essential minerals such as potassium.

♦ Beware of too much fruit juice! Fruit juice is fruit in concentrated form, with its fiber removed. Drinking a glass of orange juice takes no effort. Eating your way through the equivalent of two or three oranges is much harder. The calories are the same!

NUTRITION TIP

Red or white meat? It seems that the color of cooked meat has no bearing on its fat and cholesterol content. Some of the leanest meats such as venison, buffalo and kangaroo are deep red in color and their lack of fat has made them more difficult to cook without becoming tough!

NUTRITION TIPS

♦ Dried fruit needs to be carefully counted by anyone with a weight problem. During dying, the fruit's water is largely removed which concentrates the calories remaining.

♦ Remember: two dried apricots were originally one fresh apricot; one prune is equivalent to one plum; a handful of raisins is equivalent to a bunch of grapes.

♦ Apricots have the most concentrated dietary fiber of all dried fruit and supply vaulable amounts of iron, potassium, carotene, niacin and other B vitamins.

NUTRITION TIP

♦ Vegetables of the cabbage family—cabbage, Brussels sprouts, broccoli, cauliflower and turnip – are nutrition "superstars" and should be included as often as possible. Research has shown that these vegetables contain compounds called indoles and isothiocyanates which can protect against cancer of the bowel. They are also one of the best vegetables for fiber and are high in vitamin C and beta-carotene – and for only a few calories!

♦ Remember to cook vegetables as quickly as possible with the least amount of water to save these valuable vitamins. Steam, boil, microwave or stir-fry for fastest results and try to serve them as soon as cooked – keeping them warm for too long only reduces the heat-sensitive vitamins.

NUTRITION TIP

♦ Whole wheat and grain breads can keep your bowels healthy and regular. A recent study found that increasing bread consumption in elderly people (who are prone to bowel complaints) halved the sales of laxatives over a 4 month period. Eat at least 4 slices of day, choosing the high fiber over white loaves.

♦ Toasting bread does not reduce its carbohydrate or calorie value. It merely drives off water and converts some of the starchy carbohydrate to dextrins and sugars.

NUTRITION TIP

♦ Like all meats, chicken provides valuable protein, B vitamins, and minerals such as iron and zinc. Its iron content is only about one-third that of red meat, but is nevertheless well absorbed by the body.

NUTRITION TIP

♦ Frozen vegetables, picked and processed at their peak, retain most of their nutritional value. If cooked when frozen, they will have around the same food value as home-cooked fresh ones.

♦ When compared by weight, the vegetable which is lowest in calories is celery, then cucumber and lettuce. Three long sticks of celery, 20 lettuce leaves or ½ cucumber contain the same calories as half a slice of bread.

NUTRITION TIPS

♦ When using tuna and salmon canned in oil, drain off as much liquid as possible and add some cold water to the can. Drain off again and use fish as specified in the recipe. This removes over half the salt content and is handy when no-added-salt or salt-reduced products are not available.

♦ Fish can actually be a good source of bone-building calcium, an essential mineral mainly derived from milk! The edible bones of tiny fish like whitebait, canned salmon and sardines can be consumed with the flesh and provide substantial amounts of calcium.

NUTRITION TIPS

Low-salt and reduced-fat varieties of cheese are starting to appear in delicatessens and supermarkets. Salt is essential to cheese making, and cannot be completely eliminated, as it controls ripening and determines the final moisture content.

NUTRITION TIP

♦ When using commercial sauces, look for the many new "no-oil" and "fat-reduced" products now available.

♦ Check ingredients on the label; many mayonnaises are labeled "poly-unsaturated" or "egg-free", but are nevertheless high in fat.

WHICH MILK?

Most milks carry a nutrition information label on the side of their package which can help you decide the best type to buy, as there are differing names for similar types of milk in different areas.

Skim milk has had virtually all fat and cholesterol removed, while retaining a full complement of calcium, protein and minerals. It has the least fat and calories of all milks, but has a thin "watery" feel in the mouth.

Modified low-fat milks have a fat content similar to skim milk but with added calcium, protein and lactose. This gives them a "richer" taste than skim milk.

Modified reduced-fat milks have around half the fat and cholesterol of regular milk, but with a creamy taste, which most people find quite acceptable.

Soya bean milks are suitable for children who have an allergy to the protein in cow's milk or for people unable to digest lactose (milk sugar), but are not always a good substitute. Although they are free of cholesterol, they can contain just as much fat as full cream milk and, unless fortified with added calcium, are not as rich in calcium.

MILK FATS	
MILK TYPE	*FAT CONTENT*
Full-cream	4%
Reduced-fat modified	1.5 - 2%
Low-fat modified	0.15%
Skim	0.1%

BIG FAT SECRETS

HANDY FAT CHECKLIST	
the amount of fat contained in 100 grams of each food.	
Oil	100
Lard, dripping	100
Margarine, butter	80
Mayonnaise, rich	78
Desiccated coconut	63
Bacon	59
Tartar sauce	54
Peanuts, roasted	47
Salami	45
Puff pastry	36
Cream	36
Sour cream	35
Potato chips	33
Cheddar cheese	33
Milk chocolate	31
Corn chips	27
Shortbread biscuits	26
Chocolate éclair	26
Sesame bar	26
Cream-filled biscuits	25
Carob and nut bar	25
Croissant	24
Camembert cheese	24
Avocado	23
Cheesecake	22
Doughnut	20
Sausage roll	20
Beef, lamb, pork, fatty	20-25

OILS AND OILS	
FAT	*OILS*
Polyunsaturated	Safflower, sunflower, walnut, corn, soya bean, wheat germ, cottonseed, sesame, grapeseed
Monounsaturated	Olive, canola (rapeseed), peanut, avocado
Saturated	Coconut, palm, palm kernel
All oils are mixtures of the three types of fats. The type occurring in greatest proportion gives the oil its classification.	

VITAL VITAMINS

♦ Best vegetables for vitamin C are: peppers, chili, parsley, watercress, broccoli, Brussels sprouts, cauliflower and kohlrabi. These have a higher concentration of vitamin C than citrus fruit but are often overlooked as sources of vitamin C.

♦ Remember being told you must eat green and orange vegetables at dinner? Nutritionists today agree! Dark green and orange vegetables contain much beta-carotene (the precursor of vitamin A), which helps protect against cancer and is needed for vision. Carrots are the richest for beta-carotene, followed by orange sweet potato, parsley, pumpkin, spinach, silverbeet, peppers and chili.

FISHY TALES A guide to buying fresh fish		
	LOOK FOR	WATCH OUT FOR
Fillets	Fillets should be shiny and firm with a pleasant sea smell	Fillets that are dull, soft, discolored or "ooze" water when touched indicate fish that is past its best.
Whole Fish	Whole fish should have a pleasant sea smell and a bright luster to the skin. Gills should be red and the eyes bright and bulging. When touched, the flesh should be firm and springy.	Dull-colored fish with sunken eyes should be avoided at all costs.

CHOLESTEROL IN SHELLFISH	
All figures cooked, except for oysters, squid and mussels.	Milligrams per 100 g shellfish, shell and bone removed.
Scallops	61
Oysters	81
Mussels	45
Crab	74
Lobster	116
Octopus	140
Cuttlefish	199
Squid (calamari)	160
Shrimp	170-190
Average	140

CHOLESTEROL

In order to develop and maintain good health you must be able to avoid foods that have very high levels of cholesterol. If you have high levels of cholesterol you can eat some foods to help decrease this problem. Foods such as oatmeal, pears, and celery are very good selections to make and add to your daily menu. Avocados are loaded with nutrition and nutrients that can help lower cholesterol and keep blood sugar disorders under control and lower homocystein.

Remember high cholesterol content can cause you to have a blood clot, heart attack, or stroke. Try very hard to eat a balanced meal so that you can develop GOOD HEALTH.

KNOW YOUR CHEESES		
LOW-FAT	MEDIUM-FAT	HIGH-FAT
Cottage cheese	Camembert	Cheddar
Creamed cottage cheese	Cheddar	Gouda
Ricotta (reduced-fat)	Feta	Swiss
Edam	Mozzarella	Parmesan
	Reduced-fat varieties of regular cheeses	Blue-vein
		Brie
		Stilton
		Gloucester
		Cream cheese
		Colby

THE TOP TEN FOR FIBER	
Grams of fiber per average serving of vegetables	
Broccoli, $^2/_3$ cup	3.9
Sweet corn, ½ cup kernels	3.5
Potato, unpeeled 1	3.0
Carrot, peeled, 1	2.9
Eggplant, ½	2.7
Squash, peeled, ½ cup	2.4
Tomato, raw, 1	2.4
Potato, peeled, 1	2.4
Onion, 1	2.2
Cauliflower, $^2/_3$ cup	2.0
All figures refer to cooked vegetables, except tomato which is raw	

DID YOU KNOW?

♦ Oats were first cultivated in Europe in about 1000 B.C. and became well established in cold damp climates such as Scotland and Scandinavia, where other grains could not survive. They have long been used as a feed for animals and were often considered a "poor man's food" as they were cheap and filling.

♦ Muesli was first first developed by a Swiss doctor, Dr. Bircher-Benner, in his Zurich sanatorium in the 1890s. Rolled oats were soaked in water overnight and then a whole apple grated over the top. It was served with chopped nuts and yogurt or cream. A far cry from today's muesli mixes!

DID YOU KNOW?

♦ Tea is the most popular drink in the world. It has been drunk in ancient China for thousands of years, but did not reach Europe until 1610, when the Dutch began importing samples to Holland.

♦ Tea contains the natural stimulant caffeine, also found in coffee and cocoa. Depending on the variety and length of brewing, a cup of tea has 10-90 milligrams of caffeine, which is about half that of coffee. Tea also contains two other stimulating agents, theobromine and theophylline, which all account for tea's ability to relieve tiredness and act as a "pick-me-up".

BRAN FIBER
Wheat bran 40%
Oat bran 18%
Rice bran 26%
Barley bran 16%

Values are dietary fiber expressed as average values per 100 grams consumed.

"GOOD HEALTH"

LEARN ABOUT NUTRITION

Food	*Portion*		*Total*	*Carbohydrates*	
	(size)		*(Calories)*	*(Grams)*	*(Calories)*
Applesauce (sweetened)	1	cup	195	51.0	190
Bacon	3	pieces	109	traces	traces
Banana	1	banana	105	26.7	95
Broccoli (raw)	1	cup	24	4.6	10
Bun (hamburger)	1	bun	114	20.1	80
Butter	1	tablespoon	108	0.0	0
Cake (devil's food)	1	piece	227	30.4	122
Celery	½	cup	10	2.6	8
Cod (baked w/butter)	3½	ounces	132	0.0	0
Cookies (choc. chip)	2	cookies	99	16.0	64
Corn (cooked on cob)	1	ear	83	19.0	62
Cornflakes	1¼	cups	110	25.0	100
Cranberry sauce (jellied)	½	cup	209	53.7	206
Eggplant (boiled)	½	cup	13	3.2	10
Eggs (boiled)	1	large	79	1.0	4
French fries	10	fries	158	20.0	75
Green beans (boiled)	½	cup	22	5.0	15
Hamburger (broiled)	3½	ounces	289	0.0	0
Hot dog (beef)	1	frank	142	0.8	3
Ice cream (chocolate)	½	cup	280	25.0	100
Jelly	1	tablespoon	49	12.7	49
Ketchup	1	tablespoon	16	3.8	14
Lettuce (iceberg)	1	cup	7	1.0	4
Milk (whole)	1	cup	150	11.0	44

Food	Portion		Total	Carbohydrates	
		(size)	(Calories)	(Grams)	(Calories)
Milkshake (chocolate)	1	cup	230	28.0	112
Onions (raw)	½	cup	27	5.9	21
Orange juice	1	cup	111	26.0	100
Peaches	1	peach	37	9.7	34
Peanut butter	1	tablespoon	95	2.5	3
Peas (boiled)	½	cup	67	12.5	48
Potato (baked w/peel)	1	potato	220	51.0	198
Pumpkin pie	1	piece	367	51.0	187
Roll (dinner)	1	roll	85	14.0	56
Salad dressing (mayo.)	1	tablespoon	57	3.5	13
Spaghetti	1	cup	159	33.7	132
Steak (sirloin)	3	ounces	240	0.0	0
Stuffing (bread)	1	cup	416	39.4	158
Sweet potatoes (baked)	1	potato	118	28.0	109
Tea	1	cup	2	0.4	2
Toast (white bread)	1	slice	64	11.7	47
Tomatoes	1	tomato	24	5.3	17
Tomato juice	1	cup	48	10.2	42
Tomato sauce	½	cup	37	8.8	29
Tuna (in water)	3	ounces	111	0.0	0
Tuna (in oil)	3	ounces	169	0.0	0
Turkey (light meat)	3½	ounces	157	0.0	0

Note: Grams of carbohydrates include sugar, starch, and fiber.

HEALTHY EATING TIPS

Eat a variety of foods.
Maintain healthy weight.
Choose a diet low in fat, saturated fat, and cholesterol.
Choose a diet with plenty of vegetables, fruits, and grain products.
Use sugars only in moderation.
Use salt and sodium only in moderation.

"PRACTICE MAKES PERFECT"

WATCH WHAT YOU EAT			
	EAT AND ENJOY	**EAT IN MODERATION**	**EAT ONLY OCCASIONALLY**
Fats and oils		polyunsaturated oils monounsaturated oils polyunsaturated margarine monounsaturated margarine low-fat spreads (limit 2 tablespoons per day for cooking and spreading)	butter, lard, suet, dripping, ghee, copha, cooking margarine, solid frying fats, palm oil, palm kernel oil, coconut oil, hydrogenated vegetable oil
Fast foods and snacks	barbecued chicken (remove skin) toasted sandwiches, steak sandwiches, rolls, pocket flat bread with lean filling (doner kebabs) popcorn, rice crackers, pretzels	hamburgers, pizzas Mexican tacos and burritos	fried foods (fries, crumbed chicken, spring rolls, dim sims, battered fish, potato scallops) meat pies, sausage rolls, pasties, hot dogs fried rice, quiche, potato crisps, corn chips (and similar snack foods)
Eggs	egg white yolk free egg substitute	egg yolks – limit 5 per week if your cholesterol is high	
Sweets and spreads		boiled sweets, fruit pastilles, chewing gum, peppermints jam, honey, marmalade, peanut butter sugar	chocolate, caramels, toffee, butterscotch muesli bars lemon butter, chocolate nut spread carob confectionery
Dairy foods	skim milk, low-fat milk low-fat yogurt, frozen yogurt low-fat cheeses (cottage or curd cheese, ricotta)	reduced-fat cheeses, e.g. reduced-fat Cheddar, feta, mozzarella, Swiss, Edam low-fat ice cream and ice confection	cream, sour cream cream cheese, hard yellow cheeses (unless reduced-fat), cheese spreads ice cream whole or full-cream milk

WATCH WHAT YOU EAT			
	EAT AND ENJOY	EAT IN MODERATION	EAT ONLY OCCASIONALLY
Grains and bread	oats, rice, buckwheat, barley, brans, wholegrain cereals, rolled oats (porridge), bran cereal, wheatgerm flour, bread, crispbread, pasta, noodles, macaroni, water crackers, filo pastry (with minimal oil)	modified cakes, biscuits and loaves made with small amounts of unsaturated oils/ margarine and whole wheat flour/bran	most toasted muesli croissants commercial pastry cakes most cookies and crackers
Vegetables and fruit	all fresh and frozen vegetables (canned vegetables preferably no-added-salt) dried peas, beans, and lentils canned beans (preferably no-added-salt) fresh fruit canned fruit (preferably unsweetened or in juice) dried fruit	avocados	potato chips and other vegetables cooked in fat olives
Fish	all fresh fish canned fish (preferably no-added-salt) oysters, scallops, mussels, crab, lobster	shrimp, fish roe, squid (calamari), cuttlefish, octopus – limit twice per week if your cholesterol is high	fried fish or shellfish in batter
Meat and poultry	lean beef, pork, veal, rabbit, game (venison, buffalo), lamb, mutton, chicken, turkey (skin removed), lean mince, lean ham, low-fat luncheon meats (pressed turkey, chicken)	liver, kidney, heart sweetbreads – limit twice per week if your cholesterol is high	visible fat on meat (including poultry skin and pork crackling), sausages, salami, pate, luncheon meats (unless lean), bacon, brains
Nuts	chestnuts	walnuts, Brazil nuts, pecans, almonds, hazelnuts, peanuts, pine nuts, macadamias, pistachios, cashews all nuts (except chestnuts) are high in fat	coconut

HEALTHY DRINKS TO MAKE IN THE BLENDER

INDEPENDENCE DAY LEMONADE

3 cups water
1 cup fresh lemon juice
1/3 cup packed mint leaves, if desired
6 tablespoons honey
1 tablespoon minced lemon peel
seltzer to taste
5 fresh mint sprigs for garnish

In a saucepan bring the water to a boil, stir in the lemon juice, the mint leaves, if desires, the honey, and the lemon peel and let the mixture cool. Chill the lemonade for 2 hours or until it is cold, and strain it into a pitcher. Serve the lemonade in a tall glass filled with ice, stir the seltzer to taste, and garnish each glass with a mint sprig.

CHILDREN'S PARTY PUNCH

3 cups unsweetened pinapple juice
2 1/2 cups fresh orange juice
1/4 cup fresh lemon juice
1 pint pineapple or orange sherbert or 1 pint
vanilla ice milk

In a large punch bowl containing a block of ice combine the pineapple juice, the orange juice and the lemon juice. Garnish the punch with scoops of sherbet or ice milk. Note: children's party punch can be transformed into an adult party punch bowl with the addition of rum or champagne. Appropriate garnishes would be orange slices, maraschino cherries or a decorative ice mold.

SUMMER VEGETABLE COCKTAIL

1 pound ripe tomatoes cut into large pieces
1 cup of cold water
2 stalks of celery, chopped
2 scallions, sliced
1/2 green pepper, seeded and chopped
2 tablespoons minced fresh basil
1 tablespoon fresh lemon juice
worcestershire sauce to taste salt
and freshly ground black pepper to taste
4 fresh basil sprigs for garnish

In a blender combine well the tomatoes with the water. Add the celery, the scallions, the bell pepper, the basil, the lemon juice, the Worcestershire sauce, and salt and pepper to taste and blend until smooth. Divide the juice among 5 glasses and garnish each glass with a basil sprig.

APRICOT CARROT COOLER

1 1/2 cups unsweetened apricot nectar
1 carrot, diced
1 teaspoon fresh lemon juice, or to taste a fresh mint sprig for garnish

In a blender the apricot nectar, the carrot, and the lemon juice until smooth. Pour the mixture into a chilled tall glass and garnish with a mint sprig.

FROSTED PINEAPPLE BANANA SHAKE

2 cups of fresh pineapple cubes
2 banana (about 7 ounces)
1 cup vanilla ice milk
1/2 cup of orange juice
1 teaspoon fresh lemon juice
2 Pineapple wedges and
2 maraschino cherries
(with the stems for garnish)

In a blender puree the pineapple and the banana, Add thw ice milk, the orange juice, and the lemon juice and blend until smooth. Divide the shake between two chilled tall glasses and garnish each glass with a pineapple wedge and a cherry.

AVOCADO BUTTERMILK SMOOTHIE

1/2 ripe avocado (cut into pieces)
2 cups of buttermilk
1 cup fresh orange juice
2 1/2 tablespoons fresh lemon juice
4 orange slices for garnish

In a blender blend the avocado, the buttermilk the orange juice and the lemonjuice until smooth. Divide the mixture among four tall glasses filled with ice and garnish each glass with an orange slice.

LEARN HOW TO STRETCH BEFORE YOU EXERCISE

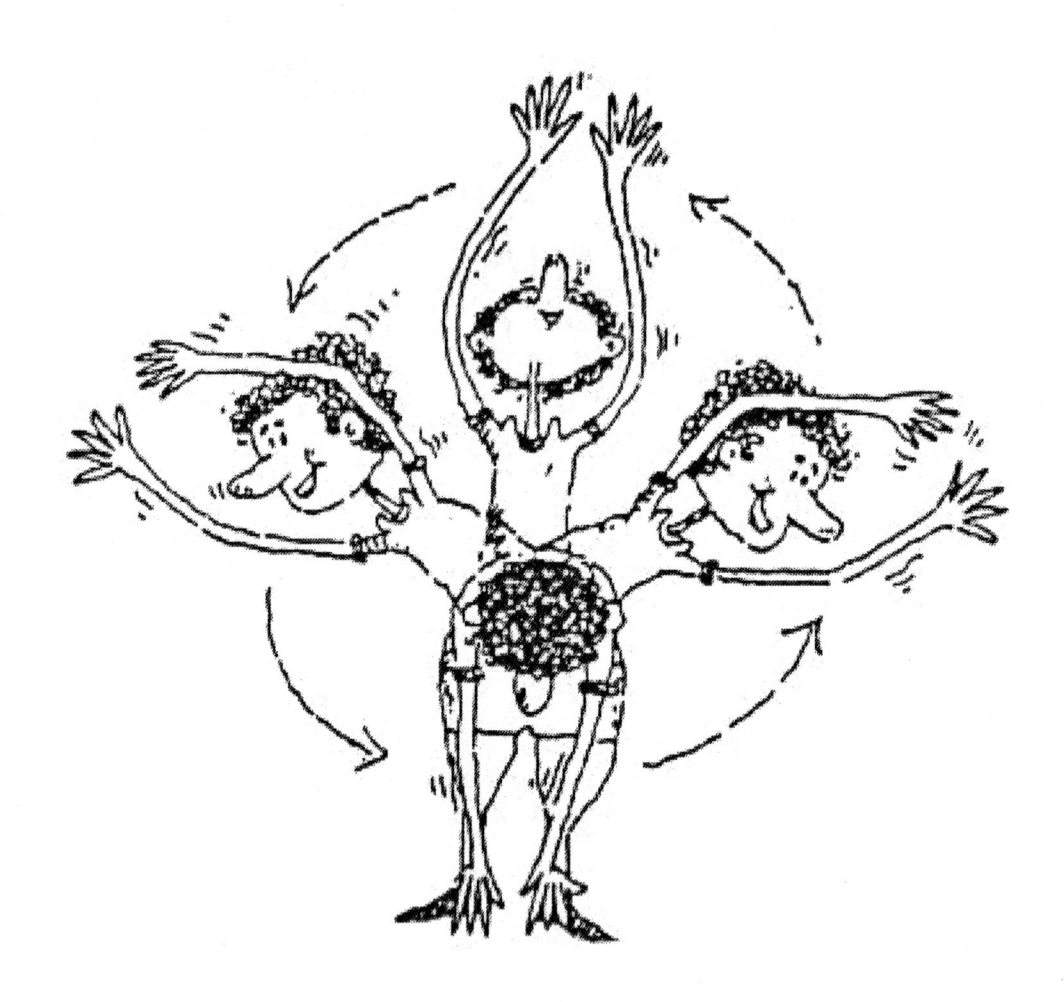

STRETCHING

STRETCHING

EXERCISE IS VERY IMPORTANT

STRETCHING

STRETCHING

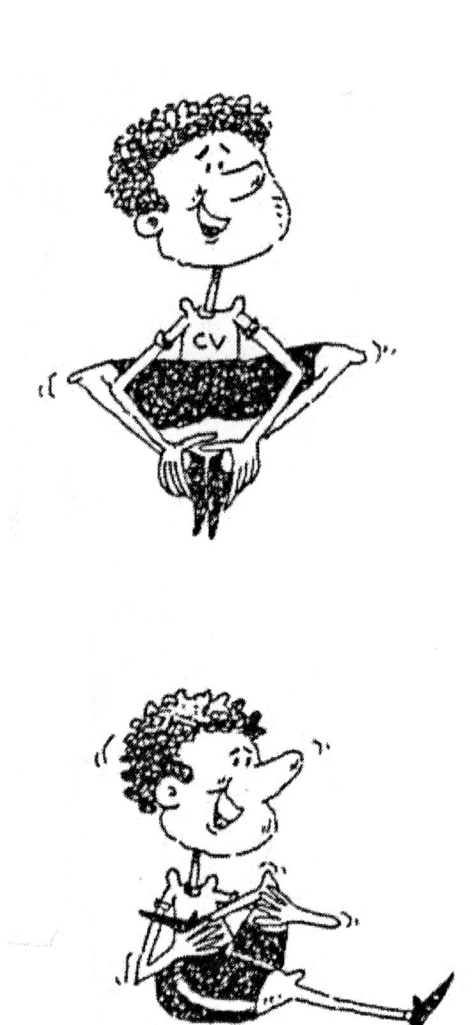

STRETCHING

STRETCHING

STRETCHING

CYCLING IS A VERY GOOD EXERCISE

If you cycle fast enough you could become the U.S.A. cycling Olympic champion.

LEARN ABOUT HEALTH AND BEAUTY AIDS

Ingredient	Products in which it is found	Parts used/benefits/history
Rosemary (*Rosmarinus officinalis*)	Shampoos, hair conditioners, scalp treatments, massage oils, bath additives, lotions, liniments.	The essential oil from the flowering stems, stimulating for the skin and adds lustre to dark hair. "There's rosemary, that's for remembrance…" This line from Shakespeare's *Hamlet* underlines the properties of this Mediterranean native. It is warming and stimulating to the skin and circulatory system which, some claim, can help your mental faculties. Nonetheless, it is beneficial to pulled muscles, bruises, and chills. It's antiseptic properties are helpful for scruffy scalp conditions.
Rose Mosqueta Oil/ Rose Hips (*Rosa rugosa*, and others)	Facial oils, creams, lotions, massage oils.	The expressed oil, and sometimes powder, of rose hips; softening and soothing for dry and mature skin types. The Swedes and other Europeans have long known the benefits of rose hips for skin care. High in vitamin C as well as B, E, and K, and tannins and pectin, Rose Mosqueta will soften and soothe the skin as well as provide antioxidant protection. A good tonic for all skin types.
Seaweed Bladderwrack/ Sea Ware (*Fucus vesiculosus*) Laminaria/ Tangles (*Laminaria digitata*)	Soaps, bath additives, facial toners, face masks, preparations for the legs, general body care.	From seaweed, extract, oil or powdered herb, softening for all skin types. Seaweeds contain algin which is soothing and softening to all skin types. They are also rich in minerals, vitamin complexes, and many trace elements that revitalize the skin and help draw out impurities. There has been some scientific research that shows that seaweed may draw radioactive strontium from the body. In days of yore, a cold poultice of seaweed was used to treat bruises and swellings.
Tea Tree (*Melaleuca alternafolia*)	Lotions, creams, toothpaste and other dental care products, deodorants, etc. Distilled oil of leaves, highly antiseptic and germicidal.	Native Australians discovered the healing properties of the tea tree oil thousands of years ago. When the first European explorers arrived, they came to appreciate its abilities to treat stubborn infections and mouth problems. Most essential oils are antiseptic septic but tea tree's high concentration of terpenes. 50-60%, makes it even more so. Does not damage skin tissue like some germicides. Tea tree prevents infections, treats mouth problems, athletes' foot, cold sores, and warts. Mildly stimulating.
Vitamins E & C	Creams, lotions, massage oils.	Commonly expressed from wheat germs and other sources; important antioxidant. E not only helps preserved products, but it is absorbed into the outer layers of the skin, restoring any minor damage and preventing damage from the elements. It absorbs very quickly and for that it is useful in helping other ingredients assimilate with the skin. (Vitamin C – and esterified C – are antioxidative skin-care ingredients; they will help the skin exfoliate, in self-repair, and in new cell production.)

Ingredient	Products in which it is found	Parts used/benefits/history
Witch Hazel (*Hamamelis virginiana*)	A flower water, in skin toners, liniments, shampoos, soaps. The flower water is an effective toner for oily or large-pored skin.	Extracts from the leaves or flower water from flower-bearing twigs, highly astringent, for treating oily skin, varicose veins, and hemorrhoids. Native Americans used the leaves of the witch hazel tree in poultices for swellings and tumors and the various uses of the plant were quickly learned by the first European settlers. It is effective in lotions and other products for leg care because it helps stimulate blood flow in the veins. Useful as a compress for treating bruises and hemorrhoids.
Henna (*Lawsonia inermis*)	Shampoos, hair conditioners, hair coloring products. In its original form it made hair a bright reddish-orange. Now it is available in a selection of colors as well as neutral, which will eventually wash away after several weeks.	The powder or extract of leaves, shoots, and twigs from the Henna shrub, will highlight natural hair color. In hair-coloring products, it coats the hair shaft with a non-sticky, flexible coating. Native a Persia, Arabia, India, Egypt, and Australia, this ancient plant provides a non-toxic way to enhance natural hair coloring by lightly coating the hair shaft, which also protects it against damage. Often used in the Middle East and India for temporary skin decoration.
Honey	Creams, lotions, skin toners, soaps, shampoos, children's products.	The sugar-based product of bee hives, soothing and moisturizing for all skin types. Wherever there have been bees, there has been honey and beeswax. And where would Winnie the Pooh be without a pot of honey once in a while? But honey, while delicious to eat, is useful as a humectant for dry skin. It contains many trace elements that help maintain good skin health.
Horsetail (*Equisetum arvense*)	Shapoos, lotions, creams, hand and nail products.	Extract of barren stems are used in products that help strengthen hair, nails, and skin. Horsetails are in a class by themselves in terms of botanical classification. These odd-looking plants, that are often found along undisturbed river banks, are one of the few plant survivors of prehistoric times; fossils of older versions have been found alongside dinosaur findings. Astringent and mildly diuretic, horsetails can help build up hair and nails and can help heal minor wounds.
Lavender (*Lavendula angustifolia* or *L. officinalis*)	Colognes, creams, bath additives, massage oils, facial toners, liquid and bar soaps, children's skin care, body powders.	The fragrant flower is commonly found in three forms – essential oil, flower water, or powdered flowers – and is soothing and antiseptic to all skin types. Lavender has been used for thousands of years to sweetly scent baths and repel moths from clothing as well as being an important home remedy for cuts and scalds, headaches, and neuralgia. Genuine lavender (there are many synthetic "lavender" fragrances) is antiseptic and mildly stimulating. Especially useful for children's skincare.

Ingredient	Products in which it is found	Parts used/benefits/history
Mints Peppermint (*Mentha x piperita*) Spearmint (*Mentha spicata*)	Foot-and-leg lotions, dental products, bath additives, skin toners.	Essential oil of the leaves; peppermint has a strong, stimulating action on the skin. The refreshing fragrance of peppermint is known to most people. It is useful in stimulating the circulatory system, hence its use in foot-and-leg preparations. Its high amount of menthol makes it also a mild anaesthetic, good for treating minor bruises and toothache. Spearmint's main constituent is carvone, containing less menthol than its cousin. It is useful as a gentle nervine and for soothing inflammations.
Nettle (*Urtica dioicia*)	Shampoos, hair conditioners, scalp tonics, body lotions.	As an extract, oil, or powdered herb; astringent and stimulating, good for oily, sluggish, or scruffy skin. The burning rash the fresh plant induces is fortunately lost in processing. Stinging Nettle, as it is sometimes called, contains formic acid, gallic acid, tannins, mineral salts, such as calcium, sulphur, and silicon, as well as protein, iron, and vitamins A and C. It is astringent and stimulating for the scalp when used in hair care products. It is also diuretic, which is useful for sport lotions and leg treatments.
Oats (*Avena sativa*)	Bath additives, facial masks, creams, lotions.	Either an extract of the seed or the chopped or powdered seed; soothing for red, dry, or mature skin. An important food crop, the ground seed has also been important in the treatment of hives and rashes and for soothing dry skin. In facial products and bath additives, it is emollient and strengthening for all skin types.
Aloe (*Aloe vera*)	Creams, lotions, facial toners, shampoos, sunburn remedies.	Juice from the leaves is mildly stimulating and toning for all skin types; has styptic (*see glossary*) properties. An African lily, this striking plant with its succulent leaves is the source for the popular gel. The pure gel is thin and watery, but it is often thickened with seaweed and preserved with citric acid to make it easier to handle. In skin products, it is refreshing and slightly drying, especially good for oily skin and treating scalds, scrapes, and burns.
Beeswax	Creams, salves, and ointments.	The wax is the remnants of honeycombs after the honey has been removed. Galen, a Greek physician from the 2nd century, used beeswax to make the first cosmetic emulsion, a mixture of almond oil, rosewater, and beeswax. This is the basis for most modern creams and lotions. Unbleached beeswax contains propolis and other elements that, in a product, help guard against infection and provide a barrier for dry skin and minor injuries.

Ingredient	Products in which it is found	Parts used/benefits/history
Calendula (*Calendula officinalis*)	Shampoos, creams, lotions, massage oils, and baby- and child-care products.	As an extract or infused oil from the flowers, good for soothing skin inflammations, styptic, antiseptic. Calendula has yellow or orange daisy-like flowers, which provide an extract or infused oil used in a variety of skin-care products. Contains calendulin, saponins, yellow resin, and a volatile oil which help with healing wounds and skin irritations. Helpful in treating heat and diaper rashes on babies and children. For the hair, helps maintain a healthy scalp.
Chamomile, German (*Matricaria chamomilla*) Chamomile, Roman (*Anthemis nobile*)	Creams, lotions, shampoos, conditioners, massage oils, bath oils, bar and liquid soaps, and child and baby skin-care products.	The flowers of both plants produce an extract, infused oil, or essential oil. German chamomile is useful in treating sprains and bruises, for sensitive skin, and for highlighting fair hair; Roman chamomile is good for dry, sensitive, and mature skin types and for children. German chamomile has a distinct floral scent with a bitter edge. It contains components which make it antiseptic as well as anti-inflammatory. Roman chamomile has a sweet, floral scent, often likened to apples.
Citric Acid	Creams, lotions, hair conditioners, bath additives.	Obtained from sugars of citrus fruits, an antioxidant and preservative, refreshing and toning for all skin types. Most cooks know that a sprinkle of lemon juice will stop cut-up apples from turning brown. It is the combination of citric acid and vitamin C in the lemon that preserves the apples. Citric acid is a popular additive to natural skin-care products for that reason. In addition, it has a mild stimulating action on the skin, helping to dissolve oil deposits in the pores.
Clay	Facial masks, body wraps, bar soap, body powders.	A powder that will help draw impurities out of the skin; good for oily or sluggish skin. Many European spas have long known that clay can stimulate the skin and help expel toxins. Clay comes from many different sources, thus varying colors, and different mineral contents. The basic action is that it will draw out excess oil and grime from the pores, toning them, and sloughing off dead cells. The minerals, depending on their composition, can help soften or stimulate the skin.
Cocoa Butter (*Theobroma cacao*)	Creams, ointments, dry skin treatments.	The seed oil of a Mexican evergreen tree; highly emollient. This is the same plant seed that, when fermented and roasted, produces chocolate. But its use in skin care won't rot your teeth. One of the few fats that will not go rancid quickly. Good for hands, feet, and elbows that are in need of lubrication, as it also contains sucrose and glucose, sugars which are humectant.

GOOD CAREERS THIS WILL ALWAYS HELP YOU

"YOU MUST ALWAYS WORK VERY HARD"

LOOKING FOR A VERY GOOD CAREER, THIS WILL HELP YOU ALWAYS

Looking for a good career is good behavior to have, you must work very hard to do a **GOOD JOB**. Please look at some of these wonderful Careers.

"YOU MUST ALWAYS WORK VERY HARD"

GOOD CAREERS THIS WILL ALWAYS HELP YOU

"YOU MUST WORK VERY HARD"

GOOD CAREERS THIS WILL ALWAYS HELP YOU

"YOU MUST WORK VERY HARD"

GOOD CAREERS THIS WILL ALWAYS HELP YOU

"YOU MUST WORK VERY HARD"

THESE ARE SOME GOOD FACES TO HAVE ALL THE TIME

Interested

Calm

Ecstatic

Cautious

Happy

Determined

Hysterical

MONEY MATTERS

Learning how to save money is a very good thing to do, your parents can help you with saving. Also use a Bank to save your **MONEY.**

"GOOD ETIQUETTE IS IMPORTANT"

TABLE MANNERS; A LIST OF THINGS THAT YOU DO NOT DO AT THE TABLE

- DO NOT: sit very far away from the table or sit jammed against the table.
- DO NOT: tuck your napkin under your chin or spread it over your breast.
- DO NOT: eat soup from the end of your spoon, but from the side.
- DO NOT: bend over your plate or drop your head to get mouthfuls of food.
- DO NOT: handle your fork and knife lightly, let the handles rest in the palm of your hand.
- DO NOT: eat very fast, take your time.
- DO NOT: spread out your elbows when you are cutting your meat, keep your elbows close to your side.
- DO NOT: try to use a fork and a spoon at the same time.
- DO NOT: feel bad if you do not eat all your food on your plate. Your plate does not have to be clean of all food.
- DO NOT: stretch across another persons plate to reach for anything.
- DO NOT: play with your Napkin, glass, or flatware.
- DO NOT: mop your face with a napkin, or draw it across your lips.
- DO NOT: try to talk with your mouth full of food.
- DO NOT: lean or rest elbows on the table.
- DO NOT: carry your spoon in your milk, juice, or beverage.

ABOUT THE AUTHOR

My name is Dr. Doris J. Brown Ph.D. Owner of Brown's Restaurant Servers Academy, located at 19376 East Ten Mile Road Eastpointe, Michigan. This is a Hospitality Vocational Trade school. I have been awarded Three Spirit of Detroit Awards for outstanding work and leadership, Three Testimonial Resolutions for outstanding work and leadership. Membership within several civic and social establishments. I have served two terms as an appointee for the State of Michigan appointed by the Governor of the State John Engler. I also serve as a Citizen Ambassador for the United States of America. I was born in the great volunteer state of Memphis, Tennessee and I now live in Michigan. Dr. Doris J. Brown is listed in the International Who's Who of Professional & Business Women. Dr. Doris J. Brown also received a Women Of The Year Award for the year of 1999. Dr. Doris J. Brown will be featured in the World Who's Who of Women for the year 1999.